Digital Home Movies

Jake Ludington

Part 1
Digital Camera B[...]

Part 2
Shooting Digital M[...] .... Pg. 14

Part 3
Shooting Digital Movies: Advanced .... Pg. 28

Part 4
Importing Video .... Pg. 36

Part 5
Exporting Video to Tape or CD .... Pg. 56

Part 6
Editing Video with Windows Movie Maker .... Pg. 66

Part 7
Effects, Transitions, and Titles .... Pg. 88

Part 8
Adding Audio to Your Video .... Pg. 120

Part 9
Still Photos and Video .... Pg. 146

Part 10
Making DVDs with Sonic MyDVD .... Pg. 158

Part 11
Share Movies with Streaming Video .... Pg. 178

Contents

Introduction 1

1 Digital Camcorder Basics 2

Identifying "Can't Live Without" Camcorder Features 4

Picking the Right Tripod 6

Using the Zoom Feature 8

Using the DV Camcorder LCD 10

Using an External Monitor 11

Extending Battery Life 12

CCDs Matter 13

2 Shooting Digital Movies: Basics 14

Planning Your Shot 16

Positioning the Camcorder 17

Properly Framing Headroom .18

Properly Framing Nose Room .19

Shooting a Wide Shot 20

Shooting a Medium Close-up Shot 21

Shooting a Close-up Shot 22

Creating an Over-the-Shoulder Shot 23

Creating an Establishing Shot 24

Creating a Cutaway Shot 25

Shooting Video in 16:9 Format 26

Shooting Video in 4:3 Format 27

3 Shooting Digital Movies: Advanced 28

Achieving Proper Lighting 30

Using an External Microphone 31

Using an External Clip-on Microphone 32

Monitoring Audio with Headphones 33

Connecting a Digital8 Camcorder to Your PC
with FireWire 34

Recording 8mm (Super8) Projection Movies with a
DV Camera 35

4 Importing Video . . . . **.36**

Connecting a DV Camcorder to Your PC with FireWire 38

Connecting a DV Camcorder to Your PC with S-Video 39

Creating a New Project in Windows Movie Maker 40

Capturing an Entire DV Tape 42

Capturing a Movie Segment 44

Organizing Your Video Files 46

Importing Still Photos 47

Importing VHS Movies with a DV Camera 48

Importing VHS Movies with a USB Device 50

Capturing Live Video 54

5 Exporting Video to Tape or CD . . . . **.56**

Preparing Your DV Camera to Save a Movie 58

Saving a Movie to Your DV Camera 60

Connecting a DV Camera and VCR for Recording to VCR 62

Saving a Movie from DV Tape to VHS 63

Saving a Movie to CD 64

**6 Editing Video with Windows Movie
   Maker** . . . . **.66**

Adding Movie Clips to a Project 68

Removing Clips from a Project 69

Adding and Removing Clips on the Storyboard 70

Removing Collections from a Project 72

Copying a Clip on the Storyboard 73

Using the Timeline 74

Adding a Clip to the Timeline 76

Removing a Clip from the Timeline 77

Preparing an AutoMovie 78

Customizing an AutoMovie .80

Saving an AutoMovie 82

Splitting a Movie Clip 84

Combining Two or More Movie Clips 85

Trimming Movie Clips 86

7 Effects, Transitions, and Titles **88**

Insert a Transition Between Clips 90

Adding Dissolves Between Clips 92

Adding Fades Between Clips .94

Adding Titles to the Beginning of the Movie 96

Adding a Title Between Movie Clips 98

Adding a Title to a Movie Clip 100

Adding Credits to Your Movie 102

Creating Custom Titles in Microsoft Paint 104

Creating Title Slides with PowerPoint 110

Adding Custom Titles to the Movie 114

Adding Effects to Movie Clips 115

Converting Your Movie to Black and White 116

Enhancing the Brightness of the Movie 117

Adjusting Contrast with Pixelan Effects 118

Applying Color Correction with Pixelan Effects 119

8 Adding Audio to Your Video **120**

Narrating a Video 122

Adjusting Audio Volume 125

Setting Audio Levels 126

Adding Audio Effects 127

Muting Audio Tracks 128

Extracting Music from CD with Windows Media Player . . .129

Importing Music in Windows Movie Maker 130

Adding Music to the Timeline 132

Trimming Audio Clips 133

Making an Audio J-Cut 134

Making an Audio L-Cut 136

Preparing the Soundtrack for Normalization 138

Normalizing Audio with Roxio Easy Media Creator 142

Adding the Normalized Soundtrack to Your Movie 144

9   Still Photos and Video **146**

Connecting Your DV Camera via USB 148
Using a Flash Card Reader 149
Importing Still Photos 150
Creating a Still Photo from Video 151
Make a Photo Slideshow 152
Adding Motion to a Still Image 156

10 Making DVDs with Sonic MyDVD **158**

Starting Sonic MyDVD 160
Inserting Movies in a DVD Project 161
Changing the Main Menu Text 162
Changing the Main Menu Style 163
Customizing Menu Buttons 164
Adding a Custom Menu Soundtrack 165
Creating Chapters in a Movie 166
Editing Chapter Titles 168
Adding Submenus 169
Adding a Slideshow 170
Burning a DVD 174
Burning a VCD 176

11 Sharing Movies with Streaming Video . .**178**

Saving a Movie for Sharing Via Email 180
Saving a Movie for the Web 182
Uploading a Movie to the Web Using SmartFTP 184
Saving Movies for Pocket PC Playback 188
Transferring Movies to a Pocket PC 190

Glossary **192**

Index **196**

Easy Digital Home Movies

International Standard Book Number: 0-7897-3114-2

Library of Congress Catalog Card Number: 2004100885

Printed in the United States of America

First Printing: June 2004

07   06   05   04   4   3   2   1

Trademarks

Warning and Disclaimer

Bulk Sales

Que Publishing offers excellent discounts on this book when ordered in quantity for bulk purchases or special sales. For more information, please contact

U.S. Corporate and Government Sales
1-800-382-3419
corpsales@pearsontechgroup.com

For sales outside of the U.S., please contact

International Sales
1-317-428-3341
international@pearsontechgroup.com

Associate Publisher
Greg Wiegand

Acquisitions Editor
Michelle Newcomb

Development Editor
Laura Norman

Managing Editor
Charlotte Clapp

Project Editor
Dan Knott

Production Editor
Benjamin Berg

Technical Editor
Tom Bunzel

Publishing Coordinator
Sharry Lee Gregory

Multimedia Developer
Dan Scherf

Interior Designer
Anne Jones

Cover Designer
Anne Jones

Page Layout
Stacey Richwine-DeRome

About the Author

Jake Ludington is the publisher of the internationally recognized newsletter "Jake Ludington's Digital Lifestyle," (http://www.jakeludington.com) which focuses on audio, video, and imaging content creation and entertainment for consumers. He is a Microsoft Windows Media MVP and contributes regularly to a variety of print and online magazines, including *PC Today*, *Connected Home*, and *MediaBlab*. When he's not writing about creating multimedia, Jake can be found creating audio and video recordings of the world around him.

Dedication

To mom and dad for giving me the freedom and self-confidence to experience life.

Acknowledgments

Thanks to Robin and Wyatt for accepting my hectic schedule. To Paul, Leisl, and Isaac for letting me invade your home every time I need to take more photos. Beth Harvey and Friedrich's Coffee (www.friedrichscoffee.com) for the photos and the caffeine required to keep me going. A big thanks to my agent, Danielle Jatlow, for professional guidance and persistence. And for all the patience and direction required to get this book out of my head and into these pages, I'm forever indebted to Michelle Newcomb, Laura Norman, and the rest of the Que team.

We Want to Hear from You!

As the reader of this book, *you* are our most important critic and commentator. We value your opinion and want to know what we're doing right, what we could do better, what areas you'd like to see us publish in, and any other words of wisdom you're willing to pass our way.

As an associate publisher for Que Publishing, I welcome your comments. You can email or write me directly to let me know what you did or didn't like about this book—as well as what we can do to make our books better.

Please note that I cannot help you with technical problems related to the topic of this book. We do have a User Services group, however, where I will forward specific technical questions related to the book.

When you write, please be sure to include this book's title and author as well as your name, email address, and phone number. I will carefully review your comments and share them with the author and editors who worked on the book.

Email: feedback@quepublishing.com

Mail: Greg Wiegand
           Associate Publisher
           Que Publishing
           800 East 96th Street
           Indianapolis, IN 46240 USA

For more information about this book or another Que Publishing title, visit our Web site at www.quepublishing.com. Type the ISBN (excluding hyphens) or the title of a book in the Search field to find the page you're looking for.

1 Each step is fully illustrated to show you how it looks onscreen.

It's as Easy as 1-2-3
Each part of this book is made up of a series of short, instructional lessons, designed to help you understand basic information that you need to get the most out of your computer hardware and software.

2 Each task includes a series of quick, easy steps designed to guide you through the procedure.

3 Items that you select or click in menus, dialog boxes, tabs, and windows are shown in **bold**.

Looking Up Synonyms

1 After you select the word for which you want to see synonyms, open the **Tools** menu and choose **Thesaurus**.

2 The Thesaurus dialog box opens. If two or more choices are in the **Meanings** list, click the one that most closely matches the meaning you want.

3 In the **Replace with Synonym** list, click the word you want to use.

4 Click the **Replace** button to close the thesaurus and replace your original word with the synonym.

Another feature of FrontPage is the built-in thesaurus that can suggest some *synonyms*, alternative words with the same meaning, for text that you've typed.

Canceling the Thesaurus
If you don't like any of the suggested synonyms better than your original word, click **Cancel** in the Thesaurus dialog box to close it.

Finding More Choices
To display a new list of synonyms based on one of the suggestions in the Replace with Synonym list, click the suggestion and then click the **Look Up** button.

Introductions explain what you will learn in each task and **Tips and Hints** give you a heads-up for any extra information you may need while working through the task.

How to Drag:
Point to the starting place or object. Hold down the mouse button (right or left per instructions), move the mouse to the new location, then release the button.

drag

drop

See next page:
If you see this symbol, it means the task you're working on continues on the next page.

End Task:
Task is complete.

Selection:
Highlights the area onscreen discussed in the step or task.

Click:
Click the left mouse button once.

Double-click:
Click the left mouse button twice in rapid succession.

Right-click:
Click the right mouse button once.

Pointer Arrow:
Highlights an item on the screen you need to point to or focus on in the step or task.

Click & Type:
Click once where indicated and begin typing to enter your text or data.

Connect:
Connect the cable to the port.

Introduction

Home movies have been part of our culture since Super 8 film cameras made amateur recording affordable several decades ago. Birthdays, baby's first steps, weddings, bar mitzvahs, and home movies capture all of the events in life we want to remember (as well as a few we'd like to forget). Today, some digital video camcorders are cheap enough to seem almost disposable, which means more people than ever are recording the events of life.

With all the special moments captured on tape come numerous shots of the camera person's shoes, shaky camera movements, and a few moments we'd all like to forget. The challenge of removing those unwanted images overwhelmed all but the most determined home moviemaker. Complicated editing software and high prices were the norm as recently as the year 2000.

Now, mini-DV camcorders and affordable software make home movie editing an affordable, delightful experience. Professional-quality editing software now costs less than $1000. Home movie enthusiasts can get started with Windows Movie Maker, which is included on every Windows XP computer. For creating DVDs, Sonic MyDVD (or something similar) is bundled with most DVD burners.

This book is your guide to making digital movies on your home computer. Between these covers, you will learn how to shoot better movies and use Windows Movie Maker to import video from your camcorder, edit your video, add special effects and titles, and save your movies in a variety of digital formats. In addition to editing digital video footage, you'll also discover how simple it is to edit all those old VHS and Hi8 movies, too. When you finish making the movie, we show you how to create DVDs using Sonic MyDVD. Even if you use software other than those that I used as examples in this book, you can still use this book to learn the basic concepts of digital video editing, and refer back to specific tasks when you need to refresh your memory. *Easy Digital Home Movies* illustrates the tasks required to easily turn home video footage into cherished home movies.

Digital Camcorder Basics

Making great digital movies requires knowing some of the basics about digital video cameras. Electronics stores tend to advertise features with exciting statistics, hoping marketing hype will reel you in to the store and convert you from gawker to DV camcorder owner. This part of the book will help direct you toward important camcorder features, while ignoring the features that just don't matter.

Basics related to use of tripods, extending battery life, and a few important camcorder features are also covered here. While the onscreen menu system found on each camcorder varies by manufacturer, the features covered are found on camcorders of all budget ranges.

This part of the book should help you make a decision about which type of camcorder will suit your needs, if you don't currently own a DV camcorder. While each feature is numbered, the features described aren't necessarily in declining order of importance.

Hardware Connectors

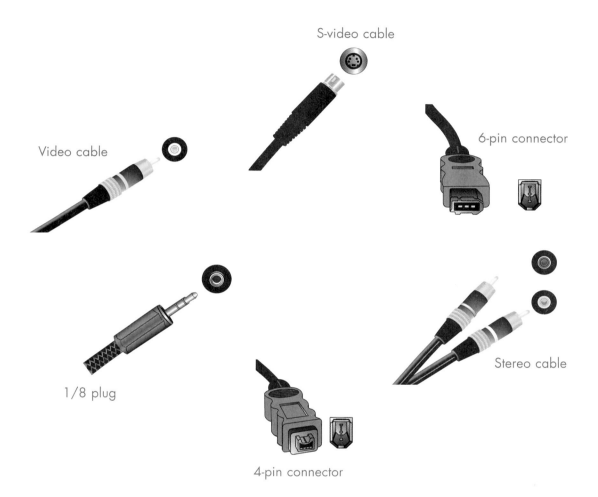

S-video cable

Video cable

6-pin connector

1/8 plug

4-pin connector

Stereo cable

Identifying "Can't Live Without" Camcorder Features

Start

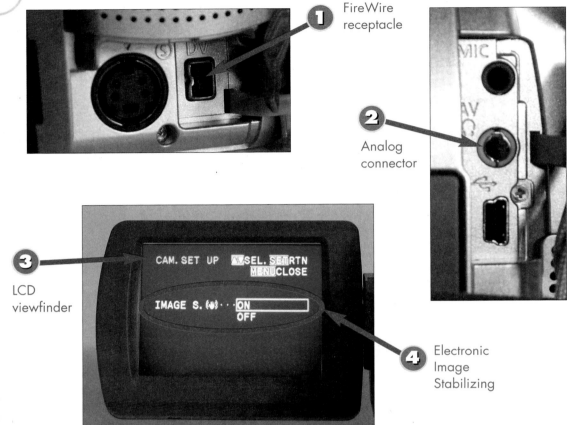

FireWire receptacle

Analog connector

LCD viewfinder

Electronic Image Stabilizing

1 **FireWire** is a must for transferring digital video from the camera to the computer.

2 **Analog connectors** are used to transfer old footage from a VCR or Hi8 camcorder to your computer.

3 **LCD viewfinders** help in framing your shot. A bigger LCD makes viewing what you record easier.

4 The **Electronic Image Stabilizing** feature (Sony calls this Steadyshot) keeps the picture from jumping around when recording with the camcorder in your hand.

INTRODUCTION

Camcorders offer more features than most users ever use. This task helps you identify features you need.

TIP

Bigger Isn't Better
While a bigger LCD screen does make monitoring what you record easier, it also drains the battery more quickly. This is an important consideration when planning to use a camcorder away from an available power outlet.

HINT

Out with the Old
If you don't have any old videos, having an analog connector on your camcorder isn't necessary. However, it will save you money on buying other hardware if you do have a collection of old media that you want to import.

Accessory shoe

6

5 Optical zoom

7 Still Camera Mode

8

5 **Optical Zoom** is important for capturing distance shots or closing in on nearby action.

6 An **accessory shoe**, sometimes called a hot shoe, is ideal for adding an outboard light or microphone to the camera.

7 **Still Camera Mode** won't take pictures as well as a digital still camera, but works as a great substitute when no other option exists.

8 A **remote**, for controlling recording when you aren't standing next to the camcorder.

 End

When to Zoom

TIP Using zoom to close in on something while the camcorder is recording isn't recommended—it might make viewers ill. Instead, zoom the shot with recording paused, and then start recording only after achieving the desired shot in the viewfinder.

Two Ways to Take Stills

TIP Most digital camcorders offer two methods for taking still images. When recording to tape, the camcorder will freeze on an image for a few seconds, often allowing the audio track to continue recording. When recording to the flash memory card, the camcorder takes a still picture just like a digital still camera would.

Picking the Right Tripod

Start

1 Smooth panning via a fluid head is a must for following action without jerky camera movement. Panning should function both horizontally and vertically.

2 Tilt is an additional feature of the tripod head designed for composing shots at angles ranging from horizontal to 90 degrees.

3 Pan handles are standard on most tripods, assisting in the production of smooth movements when following action.

4 Level the tripod using onboard leveling bubbles.

INTRODUCTION

A tripod is the most important DV camcorder feature not built in to the camcorder. No matter how steady your hand may be, putting the camcorder on a tripod will improve the appearance of your video drastically.

TIP

More Leveling Bubbles
Better tripods provide individual leveling bubbles for the leg portion of the tripod, as well as for the head portion where the camcorder actually rests. Using both bubbles will help you achieve more accurate camcorder positioning.

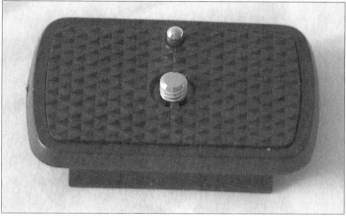

5 Hang additional weight from the center weight hook to counter the weight of your camcorder and prevent tipping.

6 Telescoping legs compact for easy carrying while expanding to achieve optimum height for camcorder positioning. Look at two features here, maximum height and closed length.

7 Adjustable no-slip rubber feet increase stability on any surface.

8 Quick release plates make switching from tripod to handheld recording faster.

 End

HINT Tripod Not Found
When no tripod is available, stabilize your body against a tree, building, or any other stationary object. Use both hands on the camera to help prevent shaky images.

HINT Affordable Stability
Tripods are manufactured using a variety of materials, including aluminum, carbon fiber, and alloy steel. Find the perfect trade-off between durability of the tripod and the resulting weight by testing models at the store.

Using the Zoom Feature

Start

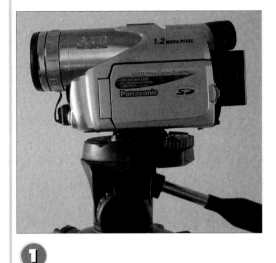

1

2 Open   **3** Turn On

4

1 Mount the camcorder on your tripod.

2 Open the LCD display.

3 Power on the camcorder in camera mode.

4 Frame the subject you want to record in the viewfinder.

INTRODUCTION

While getting the camcorder physically close to whatever you are recording is always the best option for great video quality, there are times this isn't possible. Fortunately, camcorders include a zoom feature to bring far away objects closer to the viewer.

TIP

Use a Tripod When Zooming
Zoom magnifies the image the camcorder is capturing. It also magnifies any shaking of the camera or sudden movements. To keep zoomed images looking their best, use a tripod when zooming.

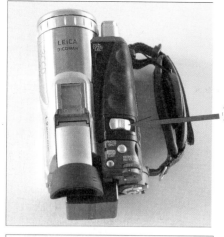

5

6

Press

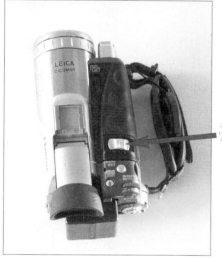

7

8

Press

5 Zoom in to the maximum optical zoom by pushing the zoom button toward the T to get a close up.

6 Notice the image quality.

7 Zoom in further using digital zoom by pushing the zoom in button toward the T again.

8 Notice the extremely grainy quality of the image, which doesn't translate to movies anyone will want to watch.

End

CAUTION

Digital Zoom Beware

Digital zoom numbers represent how large the camera can increase the size of individual pixels in an image. This doesn't actually get you a close-up shot of the subject you are trying to record. Using digital zoom can result in grainy looking video if you try to zoom in on something from too far away, as evidenced in the examples.

Using the DV Camcorder LCD

Connect

1 Monitoring recording with the LCD viewfinder approximates the shot composition of your final movie.

2 Use the onboard speaker, in conjunction with the LCD for instantaneous feedback about image and sound quality.

3 Connect the camcorder to a TV via the AV jack and then adjust brightness on the LCD monitor for a more accurate view of what the camcorder is seeing.

4 Flip the LCD around to monitor the recording when you are the movie subject.

INTRODUCTION

The DV camcorder LCD viewfinder is a versatile tool for creating great-looking movies. Using the LCD during both recording and playback helps achieve more accurate results.

TIP

Hoodman Camcorder Hoods
Glare from the sun can render the LCD viewfinder almost useless. Hoodman Camcorder hoods (hoodmanusa.com) attach to the LCD via a hook and latch system, shading the viewfinder from excessive glare.

Using an External Monitor

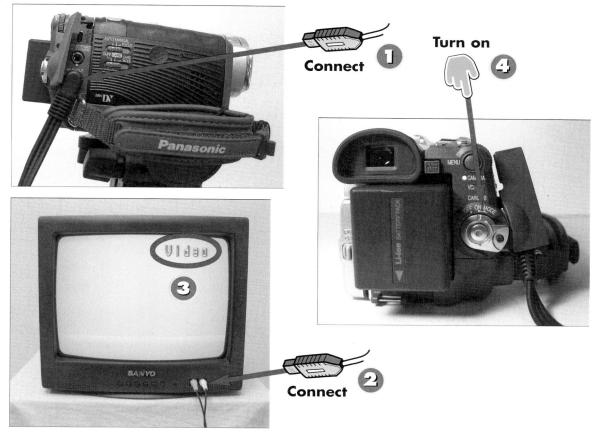

Connect ① **Turn on** ④

③

Connect ②

① Connect the mini-plug side of the A/V cable included with your camcorder to the A/V In/Out connection on the camcorder.

② Connect the RCA plug side of the A/V cable to the TV, connect the yellow plug to the video in, and optionally connect one of the audio plugs to the audio in.

③ Power on the TV and switch it to the Video channel to monitor camcorder output.

④ Turn on the camcorder to start monitoring output on the TV.

End

INTRODUCTION

The LCD screens included with most camcorders are too small to achieve an accurate sense of what is being recorded. Using a small TV to monitor video recording results in better-looking videos because you can actually see what is being recorded.

Extending Battery Life

Start

Connect

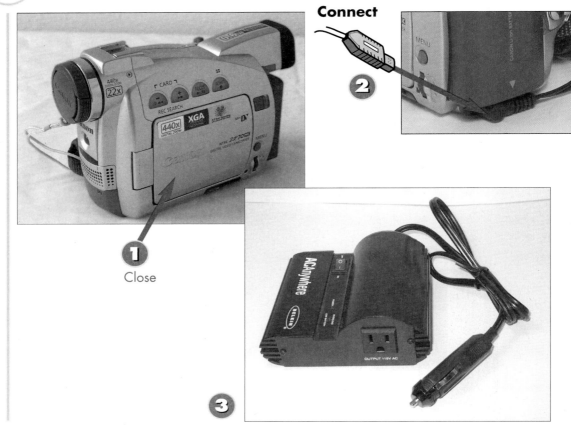

2

1

Close

3

1 Close the LCD viewfinder whenever you aren't monitoring recording. The LCD screen is the single biggest drain on a camcorder battery.

2 Plug in your camcorder when transferring video to your computer or playing back video on a TV to ensure the battery doesn't die in the middle of viewing or transfer.

3 Carry a power inverter in your car, which converts the cigarette lighter in your car to a conventional outlet, to recharge during down time.

End

INTRODUCTION

When you are capturing video, whether it's a sporting event, family gathering, or an amateur movie shoot, if the battery dies the movie is over. There are several ways to extend battery life.

TIP

Carry a Spare
Even if you minimize battery use, there are times when one battery won't be enough. Backup batteries typically last longer than the factory model and they insure you won't run out of juice early.

CCDs Matter

1 One-CCD Camcorder

2 3-CCD Camcorder

3 One-CCD Camcorder

4 Three-CCD Camcorder

1 An image taken outdoors with a one-CCD camcorder.

2 The same image taken outdoors with a three-CCD camcorder.

3 Image taken indoors in low light with a one-CCD camcorder.

4 The same image using a three-CCD camcorder.

End

INTRODUCTION

Charged-coupled devices (CCDs) are what a DV camcorder uses to capture images. One-CCD camcorders capture images by interpreting RGB (red, green, and blue) colors with one chip. Three-CCD cameras capture image data by assigning one color to each chip, resulting in more accurate color information. If you can afford a three-CCD camera, get one.

TIP

Panasonic Three-CCD Camcorders
Until March 2004, three-CCD camcorders were generally priced in a range of $1200 or more. Panasonic recently released three models, the PV-GS70, PV-GS120, and PV-GS200, starting at $699. This makes better quality video affordable for many more home movie makers.

Shooting Digital Movies: Basics

Most digital movies are of familiar things, such as family, nature scenes, or maybe a live event of some kind. Thinking about what you want to accomplish with your movie, prior to recording, will result in a better-looking final product. While it isn't necessary (or even probable) to storyboard most live recording opportunities, keeping some basic fundamentals about framing of shots and technique in mind will add a more polished look to the final production.

For the purpose of illustration, most tasks in this part of the book focus on an exchange between a customer in a coffee shop and the barista behind the counter. The progression of tasks illustrates how to effectively draw the viewer's focus to something specific within your movie, while maintaining a sense of continuity.

Getting the Best Result

Frame subjects in shot

Leave headroom

Provide room for subjects to move in the shot

Camera position

Establish location with a wide shot

Planning Your Shot

Start

1
Find
Subject

2
Frame
Subject

1 Find the subject of your movie. In this example I have captured someone making a coffee drink.

2 Frame your subject in the viewfinder, leaving room for potential movements, so zooming isn't required.

End

INTRODUCTION

Planning a shot is as simple as looking for what you want to capture in a situation and then framing it with the lens.

TIP

Art of Framing
One of the best ways to learn video framing is to study paintings. Go to the local art museum and look at paintings depicting real objects (ignore the abstract stuff). Pay special attention to where painters position people and objects within the paintings. Apply this positioning to the people and objects you see in the camcorder's viewfinder.

Positioning the Camcorder

Start

1 Steady camcorder using both hands

2 Waist level for low angle shots

1 Hold the camcorder slightly out from your body with both hands at chest height or higher for high angle shots.

2 Hold the camcorder slightly out from your body with both hands at waist height or below for low angle shots.

End

TIP

Stabilizing the Camera
When no tripod is available, get creative with solutions for getting the right camera angle and keeping it stable. Tables are generally waist high, which makes them a stable location for shooting low angle shots. A ladder is a good place to rest a camera for high angle shots, when no tripod is present.

Properly Framing Headroom

Start

1 Allow adequate headroom

2 Too little headroom

3 Too much headroom

1 Frame your subject with enough headroom so that the head isn't cut off, while not leaving the head floating in space.

2 Not enough headroom draws attention below the subject's face.

3 Too much headroom minimizes the importance of the person in the frame.

End

INTRODUCTION

Establishing appropriate headroom helps keep focus on the person you are recording. This is especially important when shooting close-ups because you don't want to accidentally cut off someone's head in the picture.

HINT

Extreme Close-Up
If you are specifically recording facial reaction, framing the face from the hairline to just below the mouth places more emphasis on emotional response.

Properly Framing Nose Room

Start

1 Allow adequate nose room

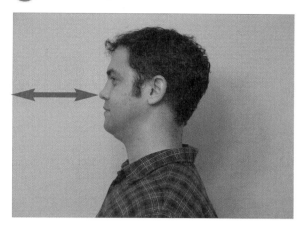

2 Too little nose room

1 Frame the subject of your shot with enough room to allow forward progress in the frame.

2 Putting the subject at the edge of the frame leaves nowhere to go but off camera.

End

INTRODUCTION

Nose room is the space between the tip of a person's nose in a profile shot and the edge of the picture. Nose room leads the subject through a frame. Leaving room in front of a person allows them move forward in the frame.

TIP

Walking Through the Frame
If you want to move a character from one scene to the next, have them walk into the frame from one side and out on the opposite side.

Shooting a Wide Shot

Start

1 Camcorder position

2 Frame the shot

1 Position your camcorder approximately 10 feet from the action to capture surrounding details in addition to the subject of the movie.

2 Frame the subject in the background, drawing focus to what's taking place where the subject is in the scene. Here you can see surrounding details about the coffee counter.

End

Wide shots keep a scene in perspective with the surrounding environment. Wide shots include background details to illustrate a location.

TIP

Adding to the Conversation
If an additional person will be walking into frame to the left, position your subject to the right of center, leaving room for the third to join the frame.

Shooting a Medium Close-up Shot

Start

① Camcorder position

② Frame the shot

① Position the camcorder so that few background details are available in frame, approximately 2–5 feet from the action.

② Frame the subject with just enough background to leave room for movement in the frame.

End

INTRODUCTION

Medium close-up shots bring the faces of people into better focus, adding more intimacy to the conversation.

HINT

Waist Up
Medium range shots generally capture people from the waist up. Just be careful that you aren't capturing only a portion of the background that won't have context in the medium range shot.

Start

Shooting a Close-up Shot

2
Frame the shot

1
Camcorder position

1 Bring the camcorder in close enough to capture the primary subject of the shot, without getting any background detail.

2 Frame the subject tightly in the shot.

End

INTRODUCTION
Close-up shots draw the viewer's eye directly to the object you want them to focus on.

TIP
Forget the Background
When taking close up shots, don't worry about keeping the background in focus. The viewer's attention should be on the face or object in the close-up, making it acceptable to have objects in the background look slightly fuzzy and out of focus.

Creating an Over-the-Shoulder Shot

Start

2 Frame the shot

1 Position the camcorder over the shoulder

1 Position the camcorder above and behind the shoulder of one party in the conversation.

2 Make the person facing the camcorder the main focus of the shot.

End

Shooting *over-the-shoulder (OTS)* of one party in a conversation puts the viewer in the conversation.

TIP

Advanced Over-the-Shoulder If an extra camcorder is available, or if you want to record two takes, also shoot a close-up of the party whose shoulder appears in the OTS shot so that you can give the viewer both parts of the conversation onscreen in the finished movie.

Creating an Establishing Shot

Start

1 Camcorder position

2 Frame the shot

1 Position the camcorder away from the scene to capture all background detail of the shot.

2 Frame the shot to include as much background detail as possible.

End

Creating a Cutaway Shot

Start

End

1 Frame the main action in a shot. In this case, dialog at the coffee counter.

2 Shoot something to shift focus from the main action, allowing for an advance in time. A close up on the coffee cup shifts the viewer's attention.

3 Return to the main action framing the current scene on camera. The barista is now making a drink at the espresso machine.

INTRODUCTION
A cutaway shot is any shot not focused on the main action of the scene. It is generally used to jump ahead in time without confusing the viewer.

HINT
Crowd Shots
One of the most common uses for a cutaway is crowd shots at sporting events. Putting in a crowd shot makes it easy to change angles without confusing the viewer.

Shooting Video in 16:9 Format

Start

2

1

1 Most DV camcorders capture video with an aspect ratio of 4:3, which is represented by the full picture extending to the outside edge of the gray bars.

2 The inside edge of the gray bars represents where this picture gets cut off when shooting in 16:9.

End

INTRODUCTION

16:9 refers to the *aspect ratio* common to widescreen movie format. Shooting in 16:9 requires planning for more room at the top and bottom of the screen.

HINT

HDTV Playback
If you own an HD television, recording in 16:9 produces video with the native HD aspect ratio. While you won't get HD quality video without an HD camcorder, this eliminates the need for the TV to stretch the picture.

HINT

Gray Bars
The gray bars in the photo above illustrate where most digital camcorders cut the image to fit the 16:9 aspect ratio.

Shooting Video in 4:3 Format

Start

1 Area captured in 4:3

2 Area as viewed on a television

1 Recording in 4:3 results in what you see is what you get movie making.

2 Oversampling by television sets, which causes portions of the video image to display off screen, means leaving important details out of the outside 10% of the screen.

End

INTRODUCTION

4:3 is the aspect ratio for normal full-screen television. DV camcorders shoot in this mode by default.

TIP

Switching Between Aspect Ratios
Use the same aspect ratio for all video clips included in one movie project. Most video editing programs render all footage to the same aspect ratio, which results in distorted video when both 16:9 and 4:3 aspect ratios are used in the same project.

Shooting Digital Movies: Advanced

This part of the book will help you make the most of elements of the recording environment you can't control, while offering suggestions about ways to get better quality audio and video out of any situation.

Without investing in an expensive three-CCD camcorder, low light is the amateur movie maker's worst enemy. Especially for digital movies, low light leads to *digital artifacts* that make your final movie look less than stellar. Knowing how to light the room for movies makes the difference between clear pictures and those shots on *60 Minutes* where the person is disguising their identity with shadow.

One of the key areas in which amateur movie makers end up losing their audience is poor audio. Hearing a person talk in a room may sound good to your ear, but what does it sound like to the camera? The built-in microphones on DV camcorders are better than nothing, but the people you are recording probably aren't going to be right next to the camera. Several of the tips in this part of the book are designed to help you achieve better audio.

In addition to improving elements of your movies, we examine advanced methods for importing existing analog footage into your computer.

Bad Photo

Too much light on owl

Shadows on bird keeper's face

Too much light on bird keeper's shirt

Person's head in shot

Good Photo

Just enough room at top of picture

No glare

Lighting produces virtually no shadows

Subject well centered in frame

Achieving Proper Lighting

 Start

1 Shadow

2 Shadow behind subject

3 Ideal lighting

1 When lighting looks like this in the view finder, try to get your subject to turn the dark side of their face toward the light.

2 A strong shadow directly behind your subject indicates light shining directly at them. When possible, diffuse the light by putting something sheer between the light and the person you are recording.

3 For most home movies, this is about as close to perfect as you could expect to get. Notice the slight shadow on the left eye, indicating light coming from my right side.

 End

INTRODUCTION

Lighting is one of the toughest aspects of movie making. Positioning the camera so that light sources act as an ally rather than an enemy of your movie is crucial to making great home movies.

TIP

Natural Lighting
Use natural sunlight whenever possible. Rooms well-lit by the sun tend to be diffused and free of most shadows.

Using an External Microphone

Start

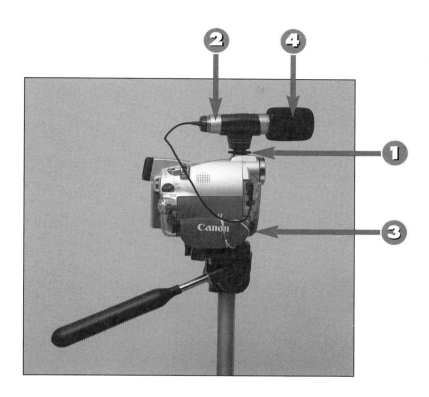

1 Mount the microphone clip in the camcorder shoe.

2 Place the microphone in the clip.

3 Connect the microphone to the camcorder microphone line in jack.

4 Use the windscreen on the microphone when recording outdoors to reduce wind noise.

End

INTRODUCTION

Using a shoe mounted external microphone results in better audio than the built-in microphone. In most cases, using an external microphone from the company who manufactures your camcorder is the best solution, although the microphones are fairly universal and should work with other models.

TIP

Operator Noise
Remember, the closest person to the camcorder microphone is the operator. Talking and hand movements will result in extraneous noise.

Using an External Clip-on Microphone

Start

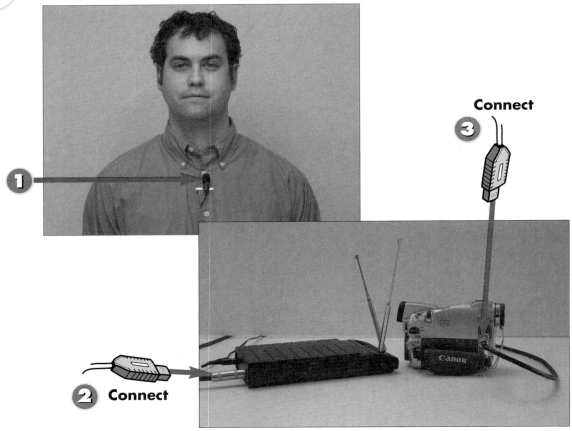

Connect

3

Connect

2 Connect

1 Clip the microphone to the speaker's shirt, just below the collar.

2 Connect the wireless microphone receiver to one end of its connecting cable.

3 Connect the opposite end of the receiver cable to the camcorder microphone line in.

End

The closer the microphone is to the source of your audio, the better it will sound. For recording interviews, putting a microphone on the person speaking is the difference between amateur video and looking like a pro.

Gain Control

Unlike the onboard microphones on many DV camcorders, most external microphones provide more control over the *gain* (input volume). Gain control lets you adjust the volume of audio up or down to improve sound.

Hide the Wire

Tuck the wire into the speaker's shirt to add professionalism to the shot by keeping it from dangling.

Monitoring Audio with Headphones

Start

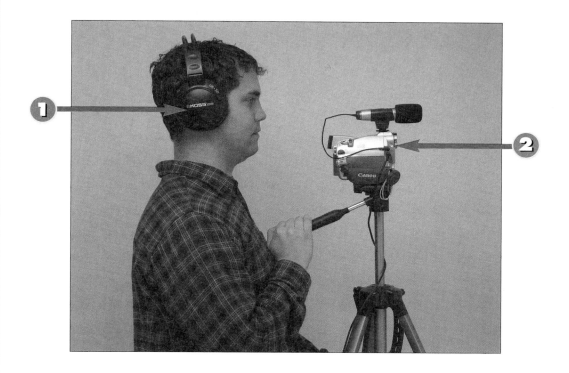

1. With an external microphone connected to the mic in on the camcorder, connect headphones to the AV in jack.

2. Place the headphones on your ears to monitor the audio being picked up by the microphone.

3. Make adjustments to the audio level of the microphone as necessary. This particular step isn't pictured because gain adjustment varies from microphone to microphone.

End

INTRODUCTION

Getting the most you can out of available audio is best achieved by listening to what the camera is recording, by monitoring audio through headphones and making necessary adjustments to the audio level.

TIP

Not Too Loud
Keeping audio from being too loud is almost more important than adjusting soft volumes. When audio is too soft, it can be adjusted louder with software. When audio is too loud, it becomes distorted and cannot be fixed.

Connecting a Digital8 Camcorder to Your PC with FireWire

Start

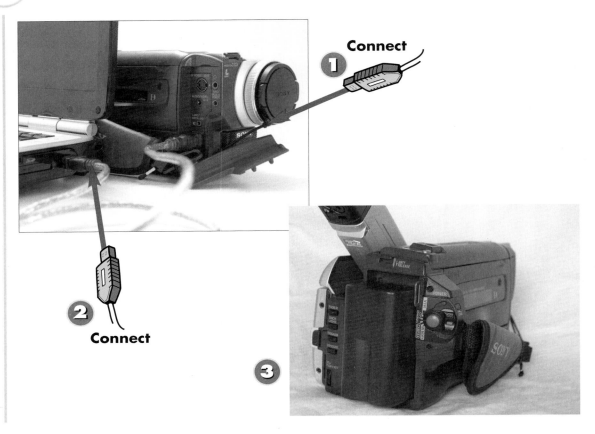

Connect ①

② Connect

③

① Make sure your Digital8 camera is turned off. Connect one end of the FireWire cable to the i.LINK port on your camcorder.

② Connect the other end of the FireWire cable to your PC.

③ Turn on your Digital8 camera in playback mode (usually VTR or VCR on the camcorder).

End

Digital8 is Sony's proprietary digital video format. To connect a Digital8 camcorder to your PC, you need a FireWire port and the appropriate cable. Most PC FireWire ports are 6-pin ports, while Digital8 camcorders have 4-pin connectors referred to as i.LINK by Sony. For this example, the Toshiba laptop pictured uses a 4-pin connection as well.

Hi8 Transfer with Digital8
One advantage Digital8 offers over the MiniDV format is backward compatibility. If you have old Hi8 video tape, you can transfer it via FireWire using a Digital8 camcorder.

Recording 8mm (Super8) Projection Movies with a DV Camera

Start

1 Set up the film projector to play the film on a screen or smooth white wall at 20 frames per second.

2 Adjust the projection lens so that the image is as small and tightly focused as possible.

3 Set up the DV camcorder on a tripod next to the film projector, so that there is minimal angle between what the DV camcorder sees and what the projector is displaying on the wall.

4 Zoom in tight on the projection, so that little or no white wall is showing around the edge of the film. When the picture is tightly in focus, start recording.

End

INTRODUCTION

Capturing Super8 film with a DV camera is one of the most affordable ways to preserve the old footage.

TIP

Recording 8mm Sound
For best results in capturing sound from 8mm film, connect the sound output on the projector to the audio in on the DV camcorder. Otherwise, you will get film projector fan noise on the entire recording.

Importing Video

Before creating the next Oscar nominated movie, raw video footage needs to be transferred to your computer for editing. Raw video footage might be in one or several formats when you start. Some of it could be on VHS tapes and some on MiniDV media used by your digital video camcorder. Using footage emailed to you by a friend or downloaded from the Internet is possible too. Still images can also be used to enhance your video. This part of the book shows you how to import any of the video clips you want to include in your movie.

Whatever the original format of your video happens to be, Windows Movie Maker needs to import it so that editing is possible. Depending on the original format of your movie clips, the process for getting it imported into Windows Movie Maker will vary. The length of time it takes to import your video depends on the length of each clip and the format it is stored in.

Getting the video clips into Windows Movie Maker is only part of the process. Importing everything from one video tape requires a slightly different process than recording only a small portion of a video tape. Once the clips are imported, organizing them into logical groups simplifies the editing process.

This part of the book explains the basics of importing video files into Windows Movie Maker.

Import Devices

Choose the video
import device

Select the audio
import device

Select the appropriate
video input source

Pick an audio
import source

Connecting a DV Camcorder to Your PC with FireWire

Start

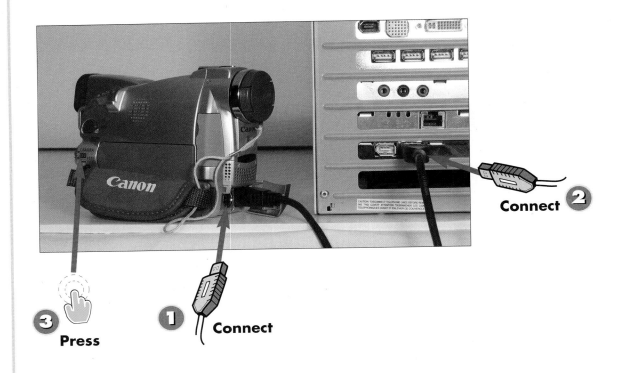

3 **Press**

1 **Connect**

Connect **2**

1 With your DV camcorder turned off, connect the 4-pin end of the FireWire cable to the FireWire port on your camcorder. (This port is sometimes labeled DV.)

2 Connect the 6-pin end of the FireWire cable to your PC.

3 Turn on your DV camcorder in playback mode (usually VTR or VCR on the camcorder).

End

INTRODUCTION

To connect your DV camcorder to your PC, you'll need a FireWire port and the appropriate cable. Most PC FireWire ports are 6-pin ports, while most DV camcorders have 4-pin connectors. If the sales person didn't sell you a 4-pin to 6-pin FireWire cable when you bought your DV camcorders, the local electronics store should have one in stock.

TIP

Other Names for FireWire
Some PC makers refer to FireWire by the technical specification number IEEE 1394. Sony refers to FireWire as I-link. All three names refer to the same thing.

Connecting a DV Camcorder to Your PC with S-Video

Start

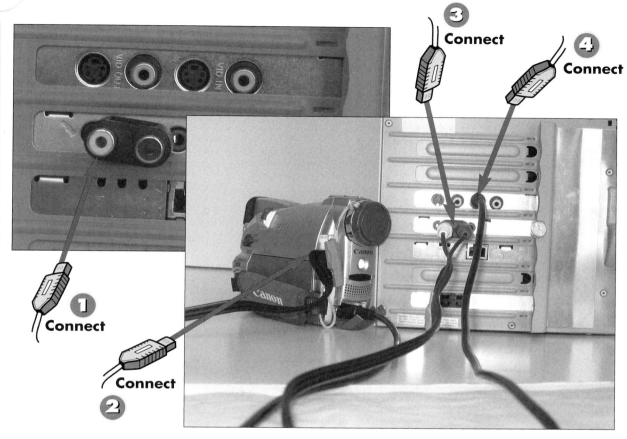

3 Connect

4 Connect

1 Connect

2 Connect

1. Connect a stereo RCA to mini-plug adapter to the line-in on the computer's sound card.

2. Connect the mini-plug end of the stereo video cable included with your DV camcorder to the AV jack on the camcorder.

3. Connect the red and white audio connectors to the corresponding jacks on the RCA adapter connected to the sound card. The yellow connector will remain unconnected.

4. Connect one end of the S-video cable to the DV camcorder. Connect the other end to the S-Video line-in on the PC video card.

End

INTRODUCTION

If connecting the DV Camcorder via FireWire isn't an option, S-Video is an obvious alternative included on many video cards. Unlike FireWire, S-Video does not capture the camcorder audio, so you will need to connect the audio separately.

HINT

S-Video Is Not Digital
S-Video produces a better quality picture than transferring video via the yellow RCA composite video out, but it isn't a digital signal. Whenever possible, use FireWire to transfer video to your computer for the best possible picture.

Creating a New Project in Windows Movie Maker

Start

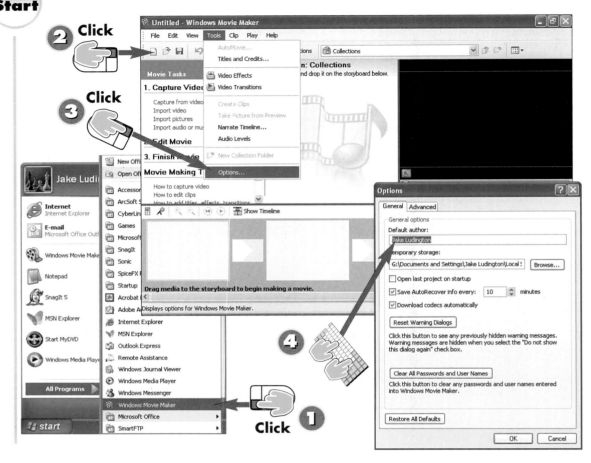

② Click

③ Click

Click ①

④

---

① Click **Start**, **All Programs**, and then select **Windows Movie Maker**.

② Click the **New Project** button on the toolbar.

③ Click the **Tools** menu and then choose **Options** to open the Options dialog box.

④ On the General tab, type your name in the **Default author** box.

Before importing your movies, Windows Movie Maker needs to be configured. These initial settings will remain the defaults for future movie projects, unless you change them. At this point, you should have already connected your DV camera to your computer.

TIP

Open on Startup
Movie projects often take longer than one sitting to complete. Open the most recent project you are working on when Movie Maker starts by checking the box next to Open Last Project on Startup, located on the General Options tab.

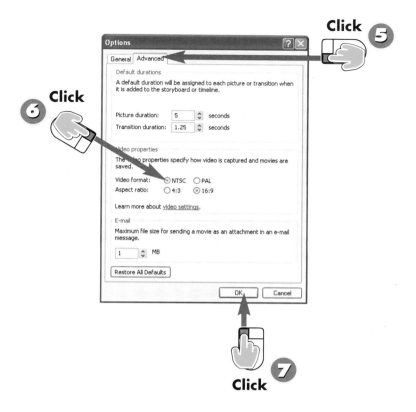

5 Click the **Advanced** tab.

6 From **Video properties**, choose settings matching your DV camera configuration.
(U.S. cameras are set to NTSC and 4:3 by default.)

7 Click **OK**.

Launch Capture Wizard Automatically
Attaching your DV camera to your PC and turning the camera on in playback mode before launching Windows Movie Maker causes Movie Maker to automatically launch the Video Capture Wizard.

Widescreen or Full Screen?
If you want to create movies in Widescreen, similar to commercial videos, set your camera to record with an aspect ratio of 16:9. Most cameras default to the full screen 4:3 ratio.

Capturing an Entire DV Tape

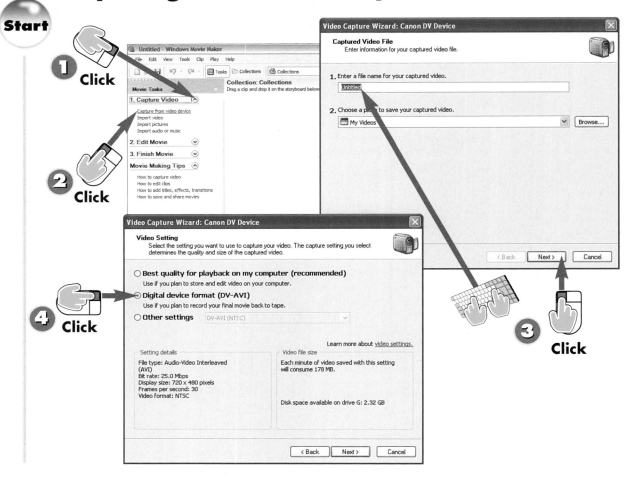

Start

① Click

② Click

④ Click

③ Click

1 Under **Movie Tasks**, expand **Capture Video** by clicking the down arrow at the right.

2 Click **Capture from video device**.

3 Type a **file name** for your captured video, make sure the folder where you want to save the file is selected (My Videos is the default), and then click **Next**.

4 Click the button next to **Digital device format (DV-AVI)**, and then click **Next**.

Before editing your movie, you need to import it from your DV camera. This process is generally referred to as capturing video. For DV tapes with one continuous event or several long events, allowing Windows Movie Maker to capture the entire video all at once is efficient.

TIP

Find the Folder
If the folder where you want to save your video file isn't the one seen in step 3, click **Browse** to locate the appropriate folder.

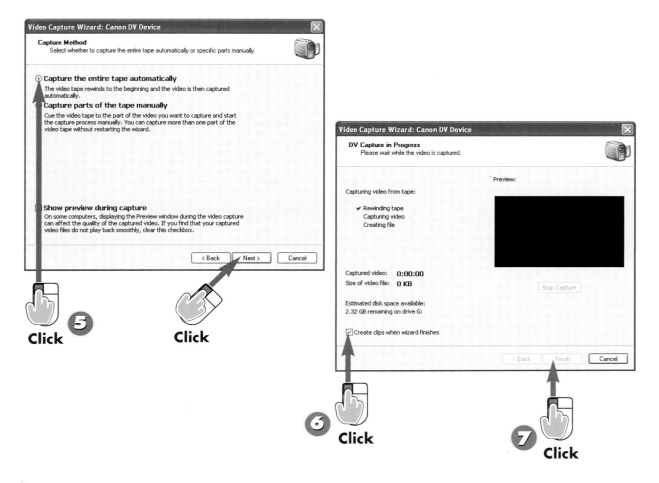

Click 5   **Click**

6 **Click**   7 **Click**

5   Select **Capture the entire tape automatically** and click **Next**.

6   Check the box next to **Create clips when wizard finishes** to automatically divide the movie into scenes.

7   Wait for the computer to rewind the tape, capture the video, and create a file, then click **Finish**.

End

Resource Hog
Turning on the Preview window during capture consumes additional computer resources, which may result in losing parts of your video. When you are capturing an entire tape, leave the Preview window off to reduce processor and memory usage.

Capturing a Movie Segment

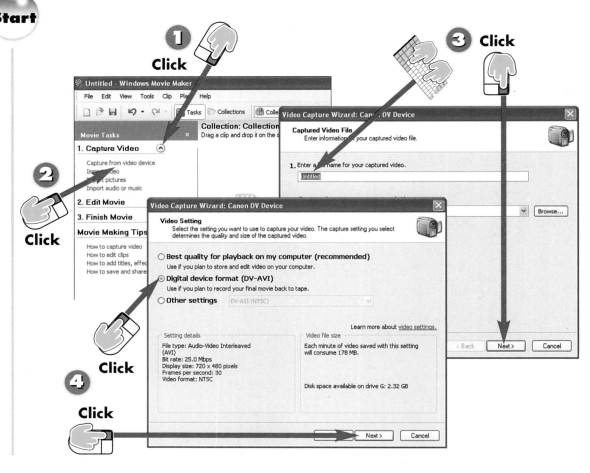

Start

Click ❶

Click ❷

Click ❸

Click ❹

Click

❶ With your DV camera connected to your PC and turned on to playback mode, click the arrow next to **Capture Video** to expand the section.

❷ Click **Capture from video device**.

❸ Type a **file name** for your captured video, make sure the folder where you want to save the file is chosen (My Videos is the default), and then click **Next**.

❹ Click the button next to **Digital device format (DV-AVI)**, which is the setting for creating a DVD later.

Sometimes only a small portion of the video on your tape is relevant to your home movie project. Windows Movie Maker lets you manually select the portion of the video you want to capture, without forcing you to import everything on the video tape.

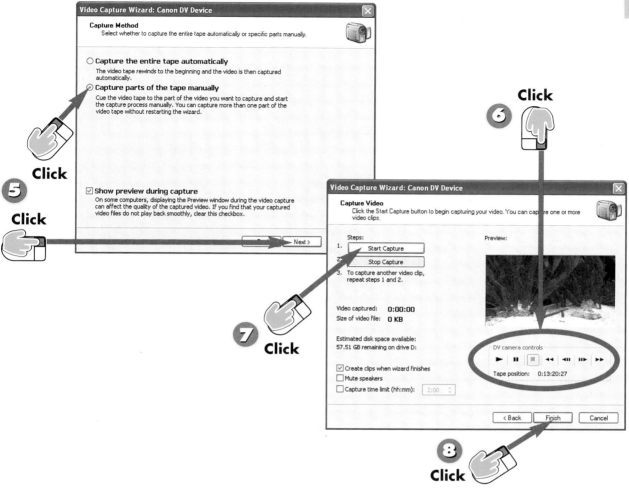

5 Select **Capture parts of the tape manually**, then check the box next to **Show preview during capture**. Click **Next** to continue.

6 Locate the portion of the tape you want to capture using the **DV camera controls**.

7 Click the **Start Capture** button and record until you reach the end of the tape section, then click the **Stop Capture** button.

8 Click **Finish**.

End

Don't Become Powerless
Always plug your camera in with the AC adapter when doing video capture. Making movies takes long enough without having to start over due to dead batteries.

Hard Drive Space
The DV-AVI video format recommended here uses about 178MB of disk space per minute of video, or around 10GB per hour. Making movies might be the excuse you need to add a new 200GB hard drive.

Organizing Your Video Files

Start

Click 1

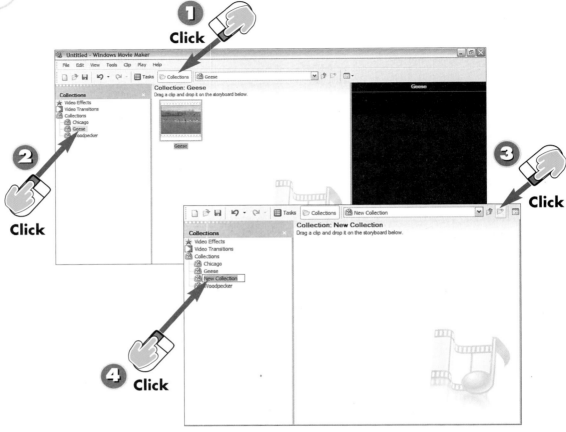

2 **Click**

3 **Click**

4 **Click**

1 Click the **Collections** button on the toolbar to view available movie clip collections.

2 Click a collection in the **Collections** window to view its available movie clips.

3 Organize movie clips by combining collections. Click the **New Collections Folder** button to create a new collection.

4 Type a name for the new folder and drag clips from existing collections to the new collection.

End

Windows Movie Maker organizes video clips in *collections*. Each time you import video clips from your hard drive or from a DV camera, Movie Maker creates a new collection for those clips. To create your own organization system, move the clips into new collections.

Repeat for All Clips
Repeat these steps until your video clips are organized according to your preferences.

Importing Still Photos

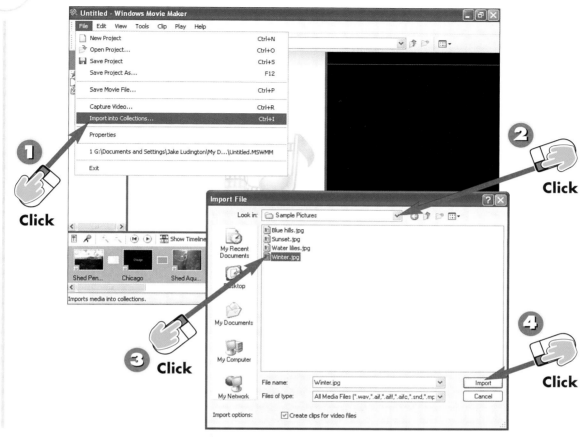

1 From the **File** menu select **Import into Collections**.

2 Click the **Look in** drop-down menu to locate the folder where your picture is located.

3 Click the picture to import.

4 Click the **Import** button.

End

INTRODUCTION

Still photos perform many functions in home movies. Photos act as great transitions between scenes. Stills make good backgrounds for titles and credits. An entire movie can consist of nothing but a series of stills set to music. The first step is to import the still into the movie collection.

HINT

Where to Find Still Photos
Still photos may be imported from your digital camera, scanned in from printed photos, or downloaded from the Internet. Just be careful to abide by copyright requirements.

TIP

Supported Image Types
Movie Maker supports most of the common image types. The following file types are the most common image formats: .bmp, .gif, .jpeg, .jpg, .png, .tif, .tiff. Movie Maker also supports these types too: .dib, .emf, .jfif, .jpe, and .wmf.

Importing VHS Movies with a DV Camera

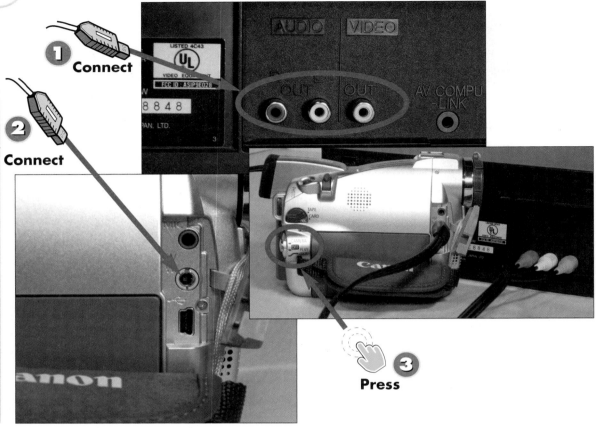

Start

① Connect

② Connect

③ Press

① Connect the red, white, and yellow ends on the video cable to the corresponding connectors on the Audio / Video Out portion of your VCR.

② Connect the mini-plug end of the video cable to the AV port on your camera.

③ Turn on your digital video camera in **VTR** (or VCR) mode.

INTRODUCTION

The easiest way to import VHS movies from a VCR to your computer is by recording the VHS tape to a MiniDV tape. Recording VHS to MiniDV involves connecting a VCR to your digital video camera. Recording the VHS tape with your digital video camera is very similar to recording a television show with your VCR.

HINT

Pass-through DV
Some DV camcorders allow you to pass an analog signal through to the computer without recording it to tape. This allows you to take advantage of FireWire transfer, without the additional step of saving the VHS movie to DV first.

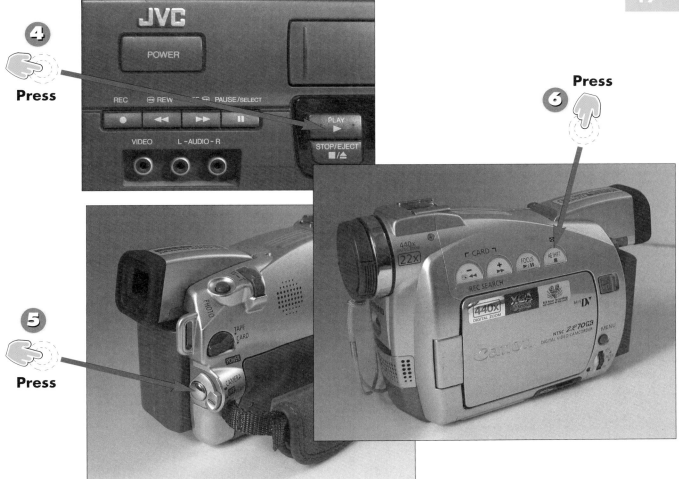

Press (4)

Press (5)

Press (6)

(4) With your source tape rewound, press **play** on the VCR.

(5) Press **record** on the digital video camcorder.

(6) Stop recording when all video has been transferred from the VCR. To import the digital video to your computer, follow the steps in the task titled "Capturing an Entire DV Tape."

End

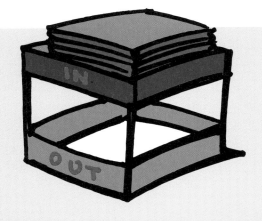

Read the Camcorder Manual
To avoid frustration, consult the manual included with your digital video camera to ensure recording from the AV line-in is enabled. This varies by camera, but in most cases, the AV port functions as both an input and an output device.

Importing VHS Movies with a USB Device

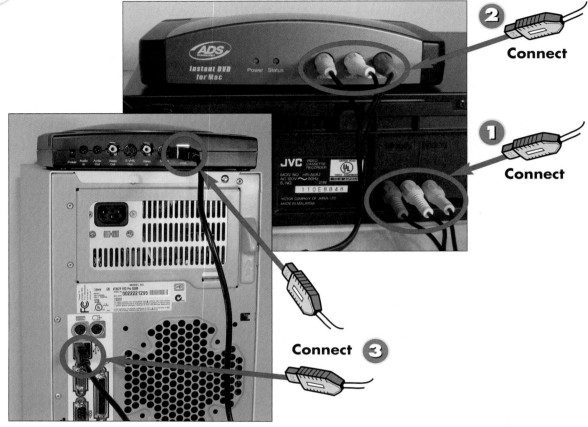

① Connect one set of red, white, and yellow ends on the stereo video cable to the corresponding connectors on the Audio / Video Out portion of your VCR.

② Connect the second set of red, white, and yellow ends on the video cable to the connectors on your USB capture device.

③ Connect the USB capture device to your computer.

Several hardware manufacturers make components designed to transfer VHS video via USB. This can be an effective way to import older video, if you don't have an available digital video camera to use. In most cases, the hardware will act as an intermediary between the computer and your VCR, without adding additional steps to the process.

Resource Conservation

TIP

Analog video capture is very resource intensive. When capturing video using a USB device, disconnect any unneeded USB devices, like Webcams, to avoid losing video frames during capture.

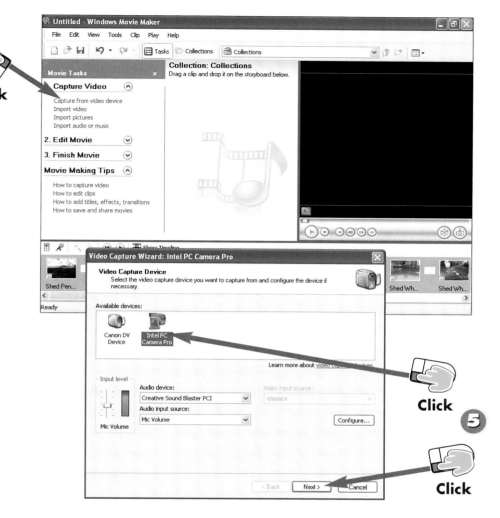

④ Click **Capture from video device** under **Capture Video** in the Movie Tasks list.

⑤ Select your USB capture device from the list of Available devices and click **Next**.

See next page

VHS or Hi8 Camcorders

These same steps work for capturing footage from an analog camcorder. Connect the video out on the camcorder to the video in on the USB capture device to transfer footage directly from old home movies. With the analog camcorder in camera mode, you can even capture live video using this USB capture method.

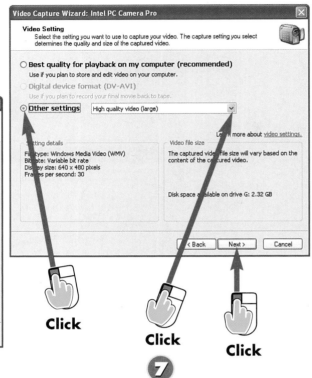

Click

6

Click

Click

Click

7

---

6 Type a name for your video file, make sure the location where the file will be saved is chosen (My Videos is the default), and then click **Next**.

7 Select **Other settings**, choose **High quality video (large)** from the drop-down menu, and then click **Next**.

Once the hardware setup is complete, it's time to prepare Windows Movie Maker to capture the raw video footage from the USB device.

TIP

Find the Folder
If the folder where you want to save your video file isn't the one seen in step 3, click **Browse** to locate the appropriate folder.

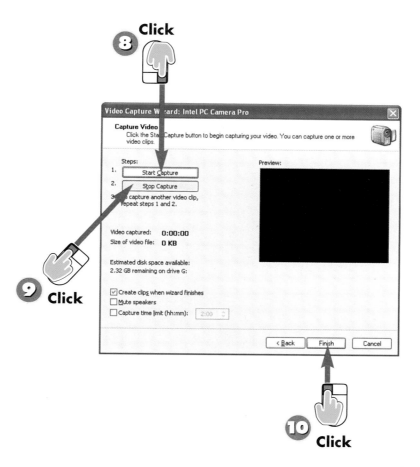

Click 8

Click 9

Click 10

8 Push play on the VCR and click **Start Capture**.

9 Click **Stop Capture** when the video is done recording.

10 Click **Finish**.

End

Analog Capture Options
TV tuner cards make great analog capture devices too. If you have the ability to watch live television on your TV, you already have built in hardware for capturing VHS video.

Analog Video Quality
Movie Maker imports analog video as WMV files with a maximum resolution of 640×480. Many USB capture devices max out at a resolution of 320×240. If your device limits resolution, choose a matching quality level in Movie Maker to prevent distortion.

Capturing Live Video

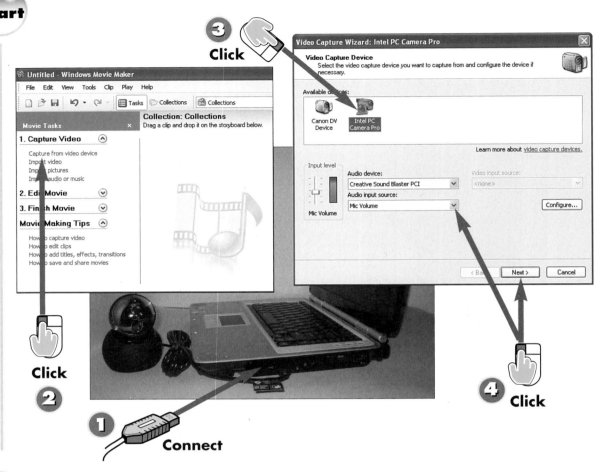

1. Connect a Webcam to your PC.

2. Under Movie Tasks, expand **Capture Video** by clicking the down arrow at the right and then click **Capture from video device**.

3. Choose your Webcam from available options.

4. Choose the **Audio input source** from the drop-down menu, and then click **Next**.

Webcams have become an inexpensive way to capture live video on your computer. Windows Movie Maker allows you to capture live movies with your Webcam for adding to your movie.

Testing One, Two...
Make sure the audio level is turned up so your voice will be heard clearly as you record the live video. This can be tested by adjusting the input level and speaking a few words.

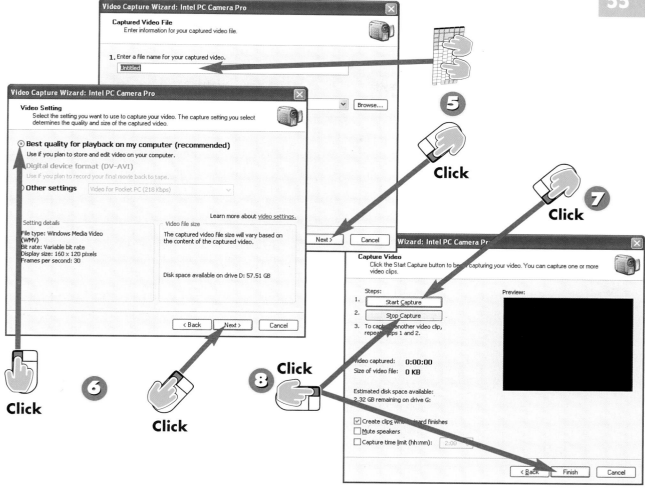

Click

Click

Click

Click

Click

5 Type a **file name** for your captured video, make sure the folder where you want to store the video is chosen (My Videos is the default), and then click **Next**.

6 Choose **Best quality for playback on my computer** and click **Next**.

7 Click the **Start Capture** button to begin recording live video.

8 When you are done recording, click the **Stop Capture** button, and then click **Finish**.

End

Webcam Looks Grainy
The camera lenses used by Webcams are tiny. A small lens means less light getting to the chips used to capture images, which in turn results in a poorer than average image quality.

Turn Off Facial Recognition
Many new Webcams now use facial recognition to track your face at it moves. This works acceptably for video chat but causes the picture to jump when recording video from a Webcam.

Exporting Video to Tape or CD

The goal of any movie maker, from home movie enthusiasts to professional cinematographers, is to output something for other people to watch. Other people may consist of your children's grandparents or it may be the audience in a local movie theater. Either way, your movie needs to be exported from Windows Movie Maker to a medium designed for playback. This part of the book examines some of the more common ways to export movies.

Similar to importing, external devices must be properly connected to the computer during export in order for the process to work smoothly. Since many people still don't own a DVD burner, this section provides several ways to share your digital movie using common solutions. We show you how to export your movie to MiniDV tape, VHS, and CD, including all the steps to achieve success in performing each of these tasks. Other sections detail the process of emailing your movie, creating DVDs, or sharing your movie from a Web site.

This part of the book offers several solutions for exporting your movie.

Output Options

Choose Your Movie Output

Save to Digital Video Tape

Save to CD

Preparing Your DV Camera to Save a Movie

Insert

Connect

1 Make sure the DV camera is turned off and insert a blank MiniDV tape in the DV camera.

2 Connect the 4-pin end of the FireWire cable to the FireWire port on your camera. (This port is sometimes labeled DV.)

HINT

Check for Updates
Video editing software periodically gets updated with bug fixes and new features. Before transferring video from the DV tape to your hard drive, check for software updates to make sure the latest version of your editing software is installed.

Connect ③

④

③ Connect the 6-pin end of the FireWire cable to your PC.

④ Turn on the DV camera in playback mode (usually marked VTR or VCR on the camera).

End

Notebook FireWire

Notebook computers with built-in FireWire connections generally use a 4-pin connector similar to the ones on DV camcorders. Most electronics stores offer both 4-pin-to-6-pin FireWire cables for standard PC ports, as well as 4-pin-to-4-pin cables for transferring movies between a notebook computer and a DV camcorder.

Cable Length

The length of the cable has no effect on transfer speed, so if you are unsure which length you need, opt for the longer cable to ensure the FireWire cable is long enough to easily reach the connection on the computer.

Saving a Movie to Your DV Camera

Start **Click** ① **Click** ②

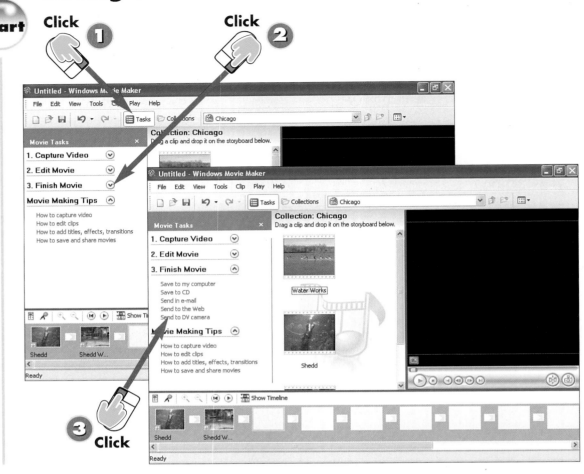

Click ③

① Click **Tasks** on the toolbar.

② Expand the **Finish Movie** section by clicking the down arrow.

③ Click **Send to DV camera**.

Windows Movie Maker automatically controls the process of saving your movie to DV tape using a built-in wizard. The wizard steps you through the configuration process. Assuming you followed the steps in the previous task, "Preparing your DV Camera to Save a Movie," saving to DV tape should work seamlessly.

HINT

Use a New DV Tape
Use a new tape when transferring a finished movie from Movie Maker. This allows the original raw footage to be archived on the tape you used to shoot the footage, while also making sure nothing embarrassing is left on the tape at the end of the finished movie.

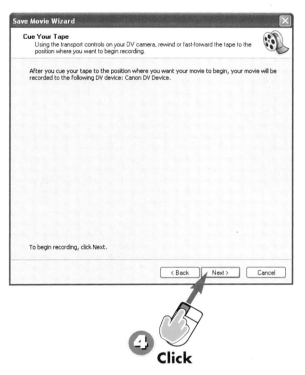

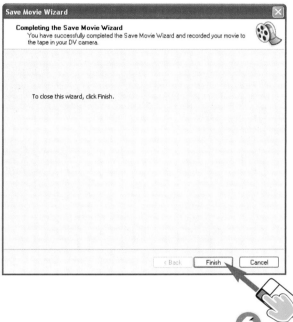

4. Verify you have a tape in your DV camera, the camera is set to VTR mode, and the tape is at the point where you want to begin recording. Click **Next** on the **Cue Your Tape** screen of the Save Movie Wizard.

5. Answer **Yes** to the warning message if you are ready to record your movie to the MiniDV tape in your camera.

6. Click **Finish** when the transfer from computer to tape is complete.

End

HINT

Use the AC Power
Plug your DV camera in using the power cable while the movie is being saved to tape. Depending on the speed of your computer, the process may take more time than your battery has available life. If the battery dies in the middle of the save process, you will have to start over from the beginning.

HINT

Close Programs
Before saving a movie in any format, it's best to close any extra programs that might be open, including browser windows and email clients. Closing programs helps free up resources for use by the video editing application.

Connecting a DV Camera and VCR for Recording to VCR

Start

Connect

Turn on

① Connect the red, white, and yellow ends on the stereo video cable supplied with your digital video camera to the corresponding connectors on the Video In section of your VCR.

② Connect the mini-plug end of the video cable to the AV port on your camera.

③ Turn on your digital video camera in VTR (or VCR) mode. Verify the correct tape is inserted in the DV camera and rewind it.

End

TIP

Color Connections
If your VCR doesn't have color coded receptacles, the yellow cable always connects to Video In. To properly connect the left and right audio signals, just remember right and red both start with the letter R, making white the left channel.

Saving a Movie from DV Tape to VHS

Start

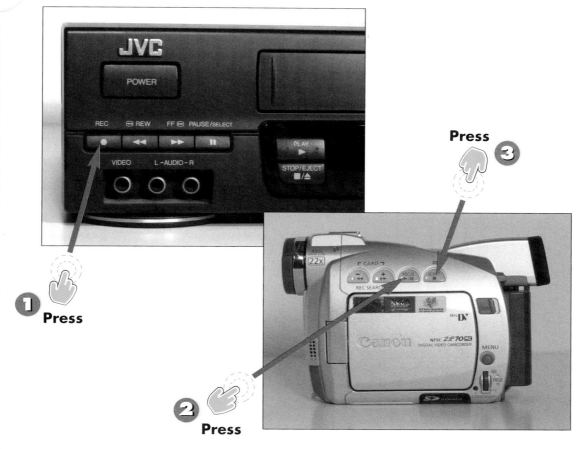

Press **3**

1 **Press**

2 **Press**

1 Insert a blank tape in the VCR and press **Record** on the VCR.

2 Press play on the DV camera.

3 Stop recording when all video has been transferred from the DV camera.

End

INTRODUCTION

Recording a movie from your DV camera is just like copying a tape between two VCRs. The DV camera is the source; the VCR records the source information to tape. Once the appropriate connections have been made, the transfer process is essentially automatic.

Saving a Movie to CD

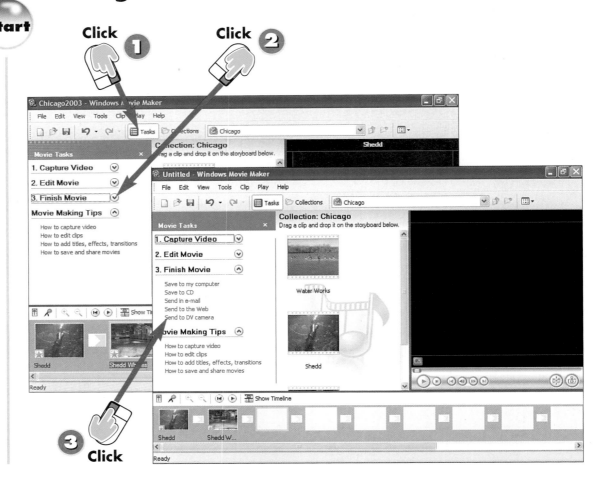

Start

Click 1

Click 2

3 **Click**

1 Click **Tasks** on the toolbar.

2 Expand the **Finish Movie** section by clicking the down arrow.

3 Click **Send to DV camera**.

INTRODUCTION

Saving a movie to CD is great for storing a backup or sharing with friends and relatives. These CDs are playable on any Windows computer with Windows Media player, as well as any consumer electronics device supporting the HighMAT format.

TIP

HighMAT Format
HighMAT is an information organization format for devices like DVD and CD players. It provides a common interface for browsing video, image, and audio files using a menu system that looks a little like the Windows Explorer. In the context of making movies, DVD players and PCs are the only devices currently supporting HighMAT. If your CD or DVD player supports HighMAT, the logo will be displayed prominently on the player.

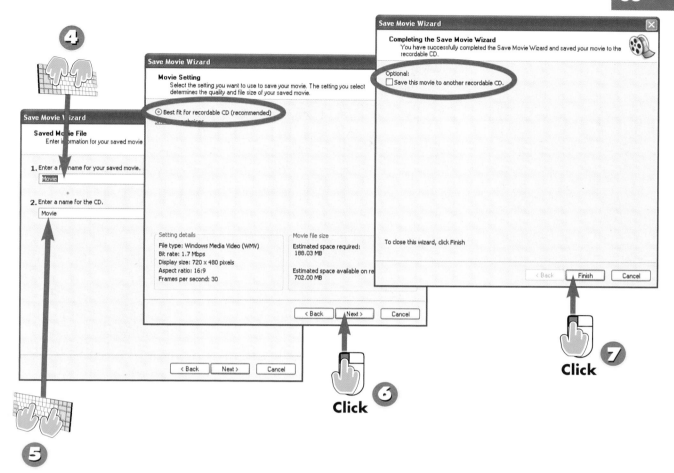

4 Type a name for your movie.

5 Type a name for the CD and then insert a blank CD-R in your CD burner.

6 Accept the Movie Setting **Best fit for recordable CD (recommended)** and click **Next**.

7 Wait for the CD to record. When recording is complete, click **Finish** to return to the Movie Maker edit window or check the **Optional** check box to make an additional CD.

Where CDs Won't Play
In general, saving a movie to CD is only useful for giving it to someone else for playback on their computer or archiving the video on CD, unless you own a HighMAT DVD player with video support.

Creating VCDs
VCD is a CD format supported by some consumer DVD players. Movie Maker does not directly support the creation of VCDs. To create a VCD, save the finished movie as a DV-AVI file to the computer's hard drive and use the directions for creating a VCD in Part 10 of this book on Sonic MyDVD.

Editing Video with Windows Movie Maker

Editing video is an organizational process involving the creation of a story from your raw video footage. Editing helps you eliminate the moments where the DV camera was pointed at your shoes, in addition to creating a logical flow of events. Editing can be as simple as choosing not to include specific video clips in your final movie, or it can be a complex process of trimming sections of each clip to build a better story. This part of the book leads you through the editing process.

Windows Movie Maker simplifies editing by making the process visually oriented. Your movie is outlined using the Storyboard and then fine-tuned using the Timeline. Each editing view offers specific strengths designed to make creating a solid visual story. The Storyboard allows you to rapidly build the sequence of events by inserting video clips in the order they should appear. Transitions between clips and visual effects are quickly added to the movie using the Storyboard view, creating a rough draft of the final movie presentation.

Switching to the Timeline, video clips are trimmed to remove unwanted material, sections of video may be divided to isolate specific content, and all of the little details used to turn raw video into a professional-looking movie are added. In this part of the book you learn how to add additional video footage, work with the Timeline and Storyboard, and edit video clips, all leading toward the creation of an audio-visual story.

Editing Views in Movie Maker

Clear the
Timeline to
start over

Drag the
Slider to
choose
trim points

Split a video clip
into two clips

Trim the end of a
clip by dragging it

Lay out the
order of clips in
Storyboard view

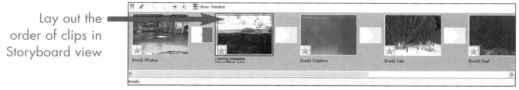

Adding Movie Clips to a Project

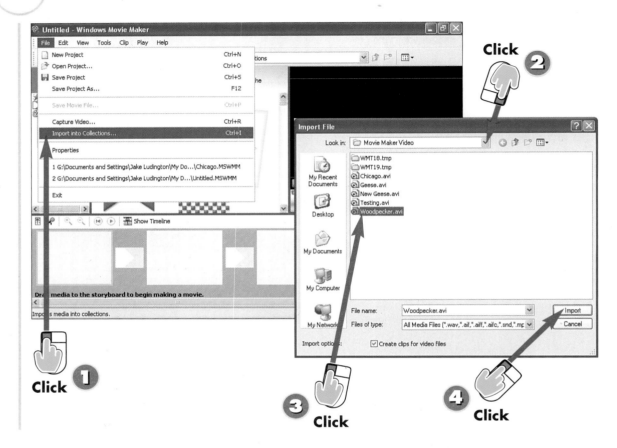

Click 1

Click 2

Click 3

Click 4

1. Open the **File** menu and click **Import into Collections**.

2. Browse to the location of your video files.

3. Select the video file you want to add to your project.

4. Click **Import**.

End

In order to create a movie, you need video clips. The clips can come from your DV camera, or be clips you have already stored on your computer. Adding clips from your hard drive to your video project allows you to use the clips in your movie.

TIP

Optional Import
In addition to using Movie Maker's Import into Collections, there is another way to add movie clips to a project. Open an Explorer window by right-clicking the **Start** menu and choosing **Explore** from the menu. Navigate to the movie clip you want to include, and then drag and drop the clip into the Movie Maker collections.

Removing Clips from a Project

Click 1

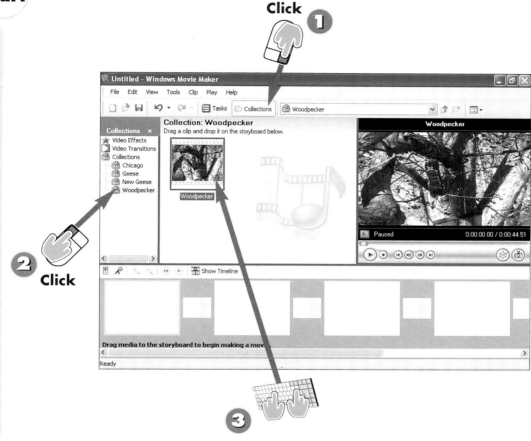

2 **Click**

3

1 Click the **Collections** button on the toolbar.

2 In the Collections pane, select the **Collection** containing the video clip you want to remove.

3 Click the video clip to select it and press the **Delete** key on your keyboard.

End

Some clips added to a project may not be used. Removing these unused clips keeps your Collection organized. Removing video clips from your project only removes them from the current Movie Maker project; it does not delete the clips permanently from your hard drive.

HINT

Recovering a Deleted Clip
Changing your mind about a deleted clip can be complicated. If the clip is part of a larger video file, Movie Maker requires you to re-import the original file, and then re-create the clip by trimming it from the section of the video file where it is located.

Adding and Removing Clips on the Storyboard

Start

Click

1

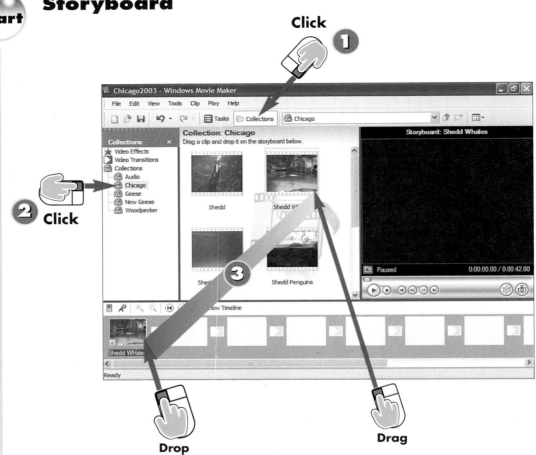

2 Click

3

Drop

Drag

1 Click the **Collections** button on the toolbar.

2 Click the **Collection** containing your video clips in the Collection pane.

3 Drag a clip from the collection to the **Storyboard**. Drag additional clips, until you have several clips for your movie added to the Storyboard.

INTRODUCTION

The Storyboard is used to organize video clips into the sequence of shots comprising your movie. Clips are ordered with the first segment of your movie appearing first in the storyboard, with successive clips following after. Adding clips to the Storyboard makes it easy to visually follow the flow of events as they progress in your movie.

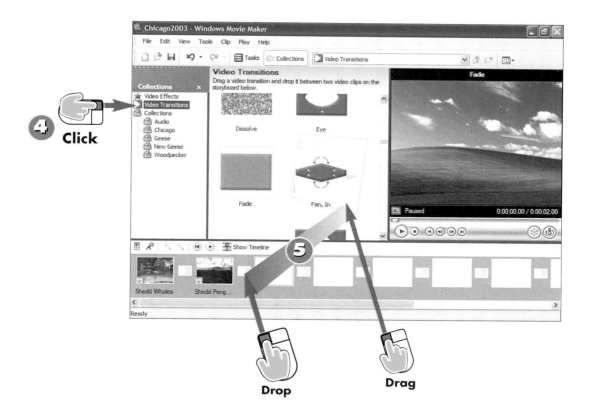

4 Click

Drop

Drag

4 Click on **Video Transitions** in the left **Collections** pane.

5 Drag the transition you want to use between clips to the transition marker between the clips.

Add All Clips
To add every clip in a collection to the Storyboard at once in the order they appear in the collection, first select one clip. Press **Ctrl+A** to select all the clips in the collection. Click and drag the clips to the first open spot on the **Storyboard**.

Repeat Clips
To repeat a video clip on the Storyboard, it isn't necessary to drag it from the collection again. Highlight the clip on the Storyboard, press **Ctrl+C** on the keyboard to copy the clip, and then **Ctrl+P** to paste it in an open slot on the Storyboard.

Removing Collections from a Project

Start

Click
1

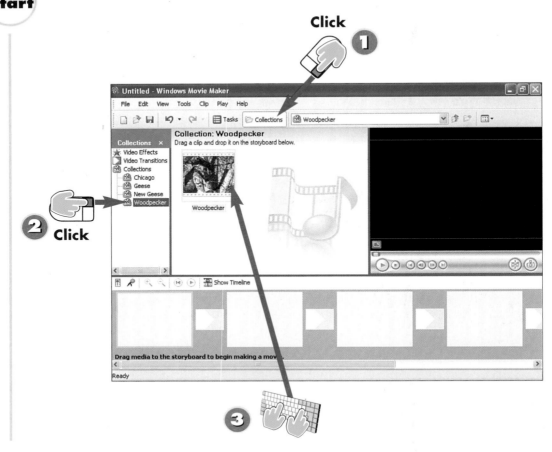

2 Click

3

1 Click the **Collections** button on the toolbar.

2 In the **Collections** pane, select the **Collection** you want to remove.

3 Press the **Delete** key on the keyboard.

End

Copying a Clip on the Storyboard

Start

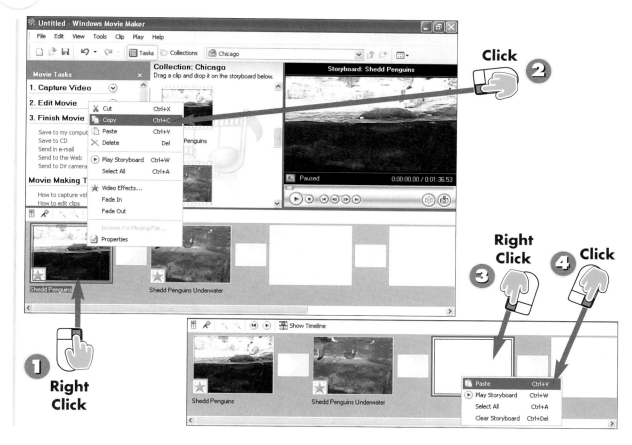

Click 2

Right Click 3 **Click** 4

Right Click 1

Right Click

1. Right-click the clip on the **Storyboard** to be copied.

2. Click **Copy** in the menu.

3. Right-click on the space on the **Storyboard** where the copy will be pasted.

4. Click **Paste** in the menu.

End

INTRODUCTION

Windows Movie Maker supports copying of clips to make repeating sections of your movie easy. Copying a clip allows you to repeat it in a loop, or paste it further along the storyboard to reintroduce it later in the movie.

Using the Timeline

Start

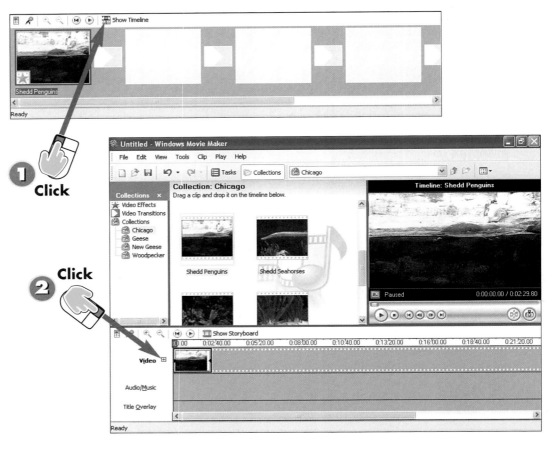

① **Click**

② **Click**

① Click the **Show Timeline** button above the Storyboard to switch to Timeline View.

② Expand the detailed **Video** view to expose **Transitions** and **Audio** by clicking the **+** next to **Video** on the **Timeline**.

INTRODUCTION

The Timeline is a detailed view of your movie. It shows the length of each clip, shows where transitions and effects overlap the clips, and lets you make adjustments accordingly. Additionally, most audio editing in Windows Movie Maker happens from the Timeline view.

TIP

Fade In
Movie Maker doesn't support using a transition at the beginning of a movie. To introduce the first scene of your movie gradually, right-click the first movie clip on the Timeline and choose **Fade In** from the list of options.

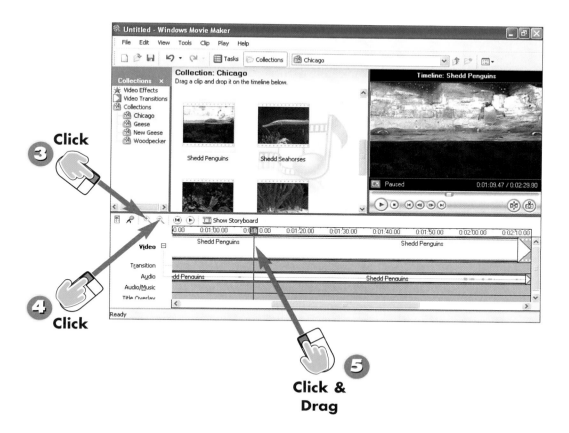

Click

3

4

Click

5

Click & Drag

3 Zoom in on the Timeline to select a more precise section of video by clicking on the **+ magnifying glass**.

4 Zoom out to gain a broad picture of your project by clicking the **- magnifying glass**.

5 Move to a specific frame in your movie by adjusting the **slider** on the Timeline.

End

Timeline Fading
Create a fade between two video clips on the Timeline by dragging the beginning of one clip over the last few seconds of the preceding clip. Movie Maker will automatically fade out the first clip as the second clip fades in.

Adjusting Timeline View
Because the Timeline contains a great deal of information, it is often easier to work with movie and audio clips by increasing the size of the Timeline. To increase its size, hover the mouse pointer over the blue line separating the collections from the Timeline until you see a double-ended arrow. Click and drag the line toward the top of the screen until the Timeline is adjusted to a size where all sections are easily visible.

Adding a Clip to the Timeline

Start

Click
1

Drag

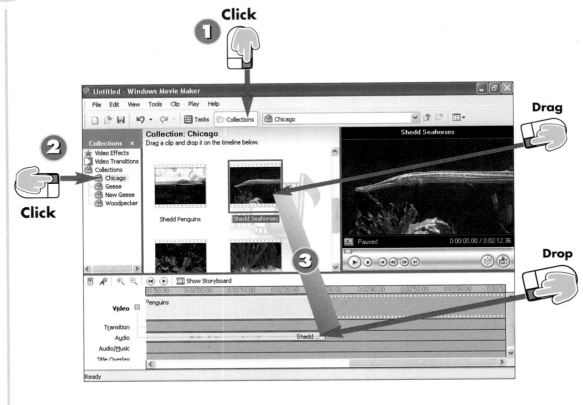

2
Click

3

Drop

1 Click the **Collections** button.

2 In the **Collections** pane, select the Collection containing the video clip to be added.

3 Drag and drop a clip on the point in the **Timeline** you want to insert the clip.

End

Clips may be added to a movie in the Timeline view, just like adding them in the Storyboard view. Dragging a clip from a Collection to the Timeline updates your movie with the new clip.

Repeat Clips
To repeat a video clip on the Timeline, it isn't necessary to drag it from the collection again. Highlight the clip on the **Timeline**, press **Ctrl+C** on the keyboard to copy the clip, and **Ctrl+P** to paste it in an open slot on the **Timeline**.

Removing a Clip from the Timeline

Start

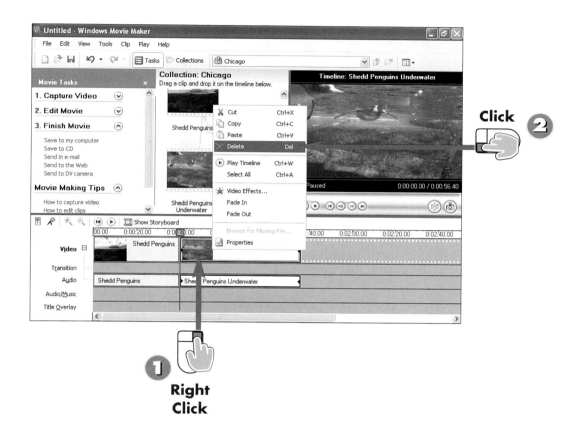

Click ②

Right Click ①

① On the Timeline, right-click on the movie clip to be removed.

② Select **Delete** from the menu.

End

INTRODUCTION

Every movie director has to make decisions about what to keep and what to remove. When a video clip no longer fits your movie, remove the clip while performing other edits on the Timeline.

TIP

Deleting Two Clips
To delete two side-by-side clips on the timeline, click the first clip, hold down the **Shift** key and press the **right arrow** key to select the second clip too. Release the **Shift** key and press the **Delete** key to remove both clips.

Preparing an AutoMovie

Start

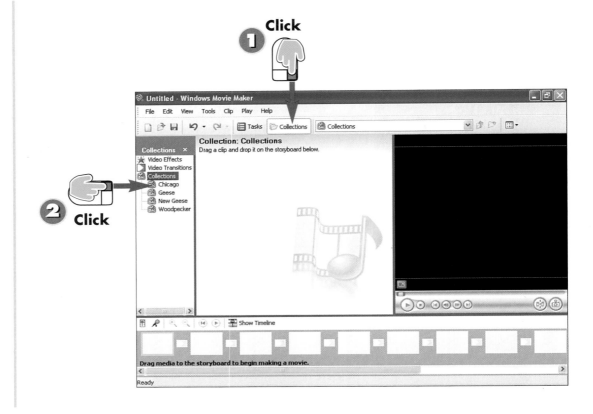

---

1 Click the **Collections** button on the Toolbar.

2 Select the **Collection** you want to use to create a movie.

AutoMovie does exactly what its name implies, automatically creating an entire movie from a selection of clips. To prepare the video clips for an AutoMovie, the clips must be selected.

HINT

Multi-Collection AutoMovie Movie Maker provides no way to simultaneously select two collections. To use video clips from more than one collection to create an AutoMovie, either copy or drag all the clips into the same collection.

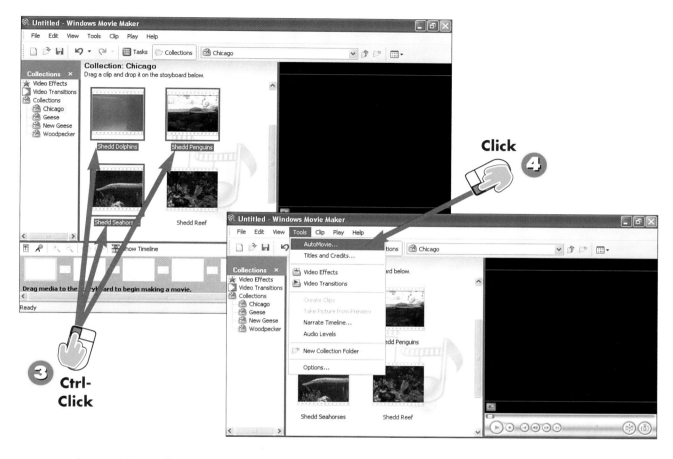

Click

Ctrl-Click

3 In the middle Collection pane where the clips are displayed, hold down the **Ctrl** key on your keyboard while clicking on each of the movie clips to be included in your movie.

4 From the menu, click on **Tools** and select **AutoMovie**.

End

Clean the Slate

TIP

AutoMovie assumes the Timeline or Storyboard are empty when you start. If there are movie clips already on the Storyboard or Timeline, AutoMovie will append the auto-generated movie immediately after the last clip currently on the Timeline or Storyboard.

Customizing an AutoMovie

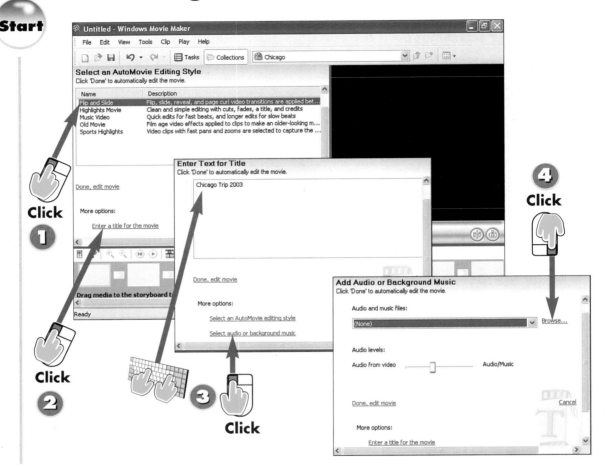

1 Select the **Editing Style** for your movie.

2 Click **Enter a title for the movie**.

3 Type your title in the space provided, and then click **Select audio or back-ground music**.

4 Click **Browse** to locate music for the movie.

In addition to choosing the video clips to be included in an AutoMovie, Windows Movie Maker offers a choice of editing style, custom audio selection, and some simple titling. For users who want to build a movie from their video clips quickly, AutoMovie is a great way to get most of the elements in place in the fewest steps. This task assumes you completed the previous task on "Preparing an AutoMovie."

TIP

Multiple Music Tracks
AutoMovie only accepts one audio file for background music. To add a series of songs, pick the first song to be added automatically by AutoMovie, then manually import the other songs by selecting **File**, **Import into Collections**. After importing the tracks, drag them to the Audio/Music section of the timeline.

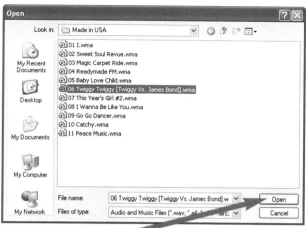
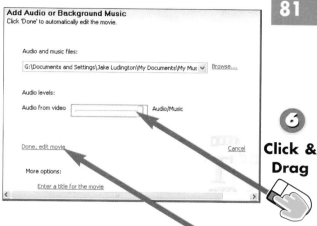

6 Click & Drag

5 Click

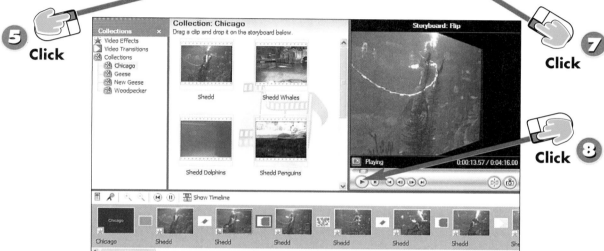

7 Click

8 Click

5 Choose the music for the movie by clicking on the file and clicking **Open**.

6 Slide the audio level more toward either **Audio from video** or **Audio/Music**, depending on whether you want to keep the audio from your movie clip.

7 Click **Done, edit movie**, and then AutoMovie processes all your movie clips, adding transitions automatically.

8 Preview the AutoMovie by clicking the **Play** button in the preview pane.

End

AutoMovie Time Limit
AutoMovie limits the length of its creation to the length of the music track selected during the customization process. If no music track is selected, AutoMovie defaults to a three-minute maximum.

Muting the Video Track
By default AutoMovie assumes you want to hear the audio track associated with the video clips as well as the soundtrack music. If you didn't mute the audio track in step 6 of this task and you decide it should be muted, switch to **Timeline** view and then select all the audio on the **Audio** section of the timeline by pressing **Ctrl+A**. Right-click the selected files, and choose **Mute** from the menu.

Saving an AutoMovie

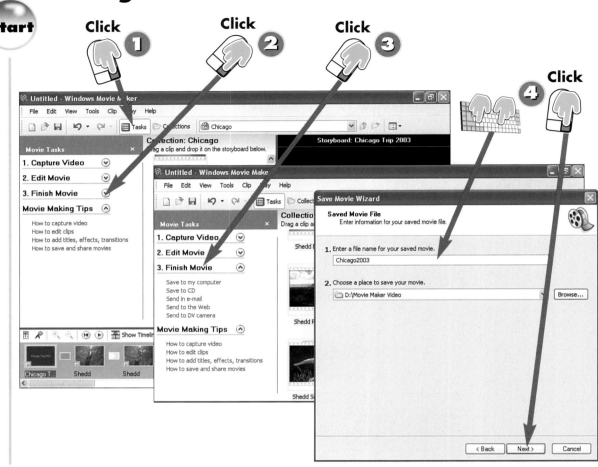

Start

Click 1

Click 2

Click 3

Click 4

1 Click **Tasks** on the toolbar.

2 Click the down arrow next to **Finish Movie**.

3 Click **Save to my computer**.

4 Type a name for your movie file and choose the folder where the movie will be saved (My Videos is the default). Click **Next**.

With an AutoMovie successfully created in the previous two tasks, it's time to save the movie. Saving the movie to the hard drive makes it easy to import the file into a DVD-creating application, burn it to CD, or save it to MiniDV tape later.

Sharing an AutoMovie via Email
The DV-AVI format is far too large for sending video via email. If you plan to share an AutoMovie with family and friends, choose one of the settings optimized for email from the list of save options.

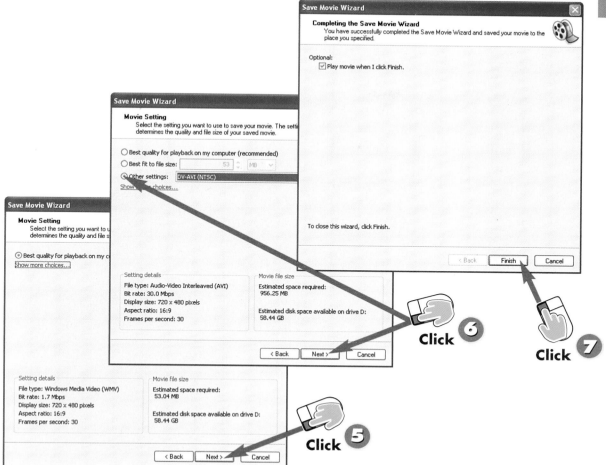

Click ⑤

Click ⑥

Click ⑦

⑤ Click **Show more choices**, to select a format. Click **Next**.

⑥ Click **Other settings**, and then choose **DV-AVI (NTSC)** from the drop-down menu.

⑦ When the movie has finished saving click **Finish**.

End

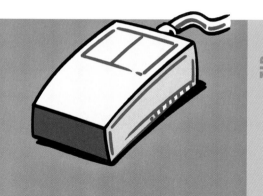

Don't Want to Preview?
Uncheck the **Play movie when I click Finish** check box if you do not wish to view the finished movie immediately.

Number One Fan
If you have movie clips and music from a favorite band, AutoMovie is an easy way to create your own music videos. Be sure you have the rights to the video or audio content before sharing a movie like this with other people.

Splitting a Movie Clip

Start

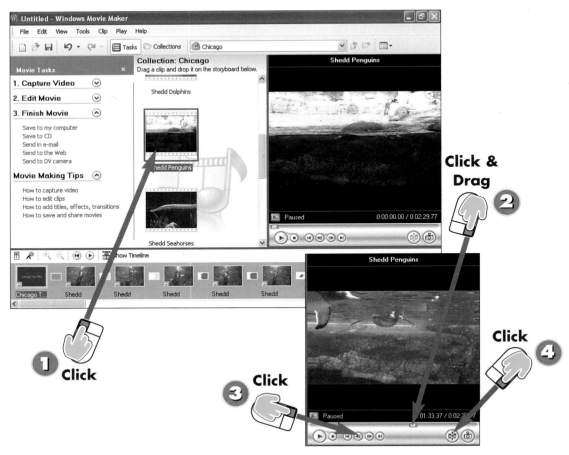

Click & Drag 2

Click 4

Click 3

1 **Click**

---

1 Select the clip you want to split from the list of clips in the **Collection** pane.

2 Click and drag the slider to the approximate point in the clip where the split will be made.

3 Use the **Next Frame** and **Previous Frame** buttons to position the clip more precisely.

4 Click the **Split** button.

End

INTRODUCTION

Splitting a movie clip into two clips lets you use the clips in separate parts of your movie. Divide the clip into two parts at the frame where you want the split to occur, making it easy to use each piece of the clip in any part of your movie.

TIP

Splitting Clips on the Timeline
Video clips may also be split from the timeline. With Movie Maker in Timeline view, use the blue slider to find the point in a video clip where a split should occur. Click the **Split** button under the monitor pane.

Combining Two or More Movie Clips

Start

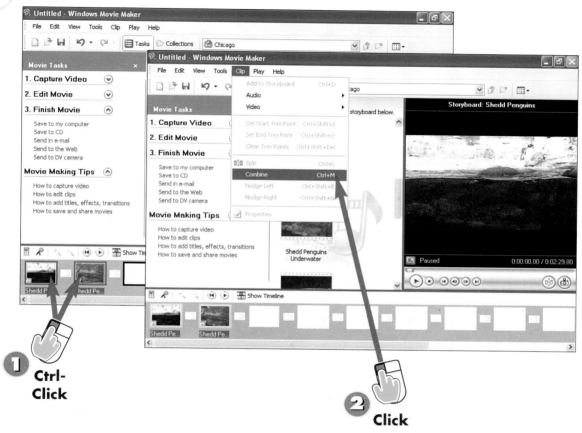

Ctrl-
Click

② Click

① Press the **Ctrl** key on your keyboard and click to select the clips from the Storyboard you want to combine.

② From the **Clip** menu, choose **Combine**.

End

Combining movie clips eliminates breaks in the flow of your video. If two video clips follow each other chronologically in your movie, combining them helps keep the story flow organized.

TIP

Combining Sequential Clips
To combine a large series of sequential clips, select the first clip on the storyboard, press the **Shift** key, and then click the last clip. When all the clips are selected, choose **Combine** from the **Clip** menu.

Trimming Movie Clips

Start

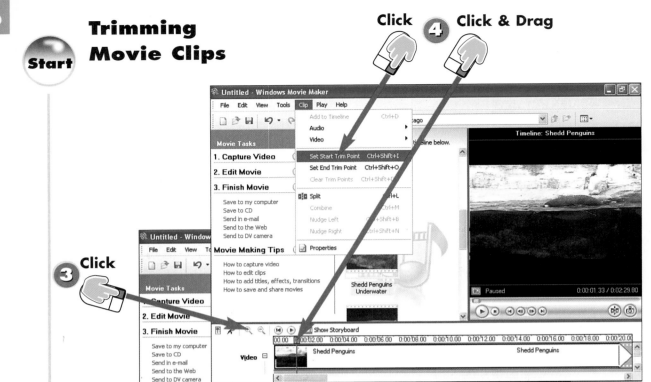

1. Select the clip you want to trim in the **Collections** pane and drag it to the **Storyboard**.

2. Click **Show Timeline** on the Storyboard toolbar.

3. Click the **Zoom In** button to stretch your clip on the Timeline.

4. Drag the **play marker** to the point where you want your clip to start, and then from the **Clip** menu choose **Set Start Trim Point**.

INTRODUCTION

Trimming movie clips allows you to remove frames from the front or back of the clip. Trimming is useful when a movie clip includes extra material on either end or contains footage irrelevant to the movie project. Trimming is most often used to remove things like unintended shots of feet, walls, the lens cap, and other obstacles to the intended subject.

HINT

Hidden Frames

Trimming a clip doesn't actually remove the video frames from the Timeline; it merely hides them. The hidden frames are skipped over during playback of the video and ignored when the final movie is saved. This effectively eliminates them from the movie, but also makes it easy to readjust trim points later without needing to re-add the full clip to the Timeline.

Click

6

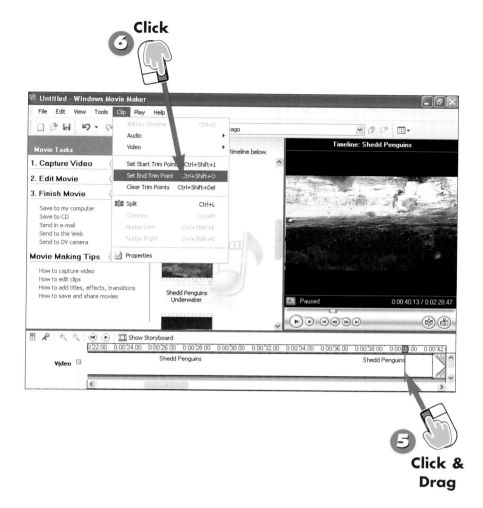

5

**Click &
Drag**

5 Click and drag the **play marker** to the point where the clip should end.

6 Choose **Set End Trim Point** from the **Clip** menu.

End

More Precision Trimming
When it seems impossible to find the exact spot to trim a video clip, zoom in further on the timeline. This makes incremental shifts of the play marker more subtle, allowing for very precise marking of trim points.

Precision Trimming
When dragging the edge of a clip doesn't result in finding the exact trim point needed, try using the Monitor pane instead. Scroll the play marker under the Monitor pane to the point in the video where a trim should be inserted. Select **Clip, Set Start Trim Point** or **Set End Trim Point** depending on which side of the clip you are trimming.

Effects, Transitions, and Titles

Once you determine the order of video clips and trim them to fit the parameters of your movie, it's time to add additional production features. Effects serve several purposes in movie making, including artistic enhancements, color correction, and unique image manipulations. Transitions are inserted between scenes, helping to identify a change in the storyline of the movie. Titles are an effective way to give credit to participants in the movie, set the scene for events within the story, or to fill in the blanks where no video is available.

Windows Movie Maker includes several transitions and effects. Microsoft includes additional effects and transitions through the release of seasonal Fun Packs. Fun Packs may be downloaded from the Windows Movie Maker site on Microsoft.com: http://www.microsoft.com/windowsxp/moviemaker/default.asp.

Bundled effects and transitions are further extended using the SpiceFX packs from Pixelan (www.pixelan.com/mm/intro.htm). 94 different effects and 74 transitions make up the SpiceFX collection, including contrast adjustments and a variety of color corrective solutions.

Movie Maker includes a selection of preset title effects, making it easy to create scrolling credits, overlay text on top of video, and animate title text throughout the movie. Movie Maker titles allow the user to customize fonts and background colors, and to make minor choices about text screen position. For completely custom titles, additional programs are required. This is illustrated here using Microsoft Paint, which ships with every copy of Windows XP. Microsoft PowerPoint is also demonstrated as a valuable title creation tool.

In this part of the book, we examine a variety of effects and transitions for enhancing movies, as well as creating titles.

Effects and Transitions Enhance Your Movie

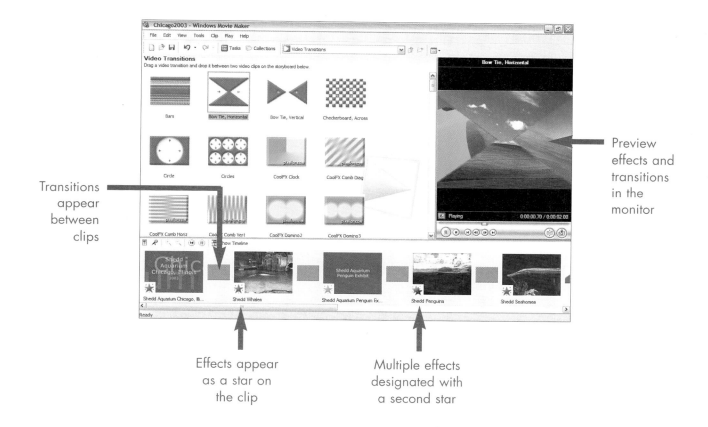

Transitions appear between clips

Preview effects and transitions in the monitor

Effects appear as a star on the clip

Multiple effects designated with a second star

Insert a Transition Between Clips

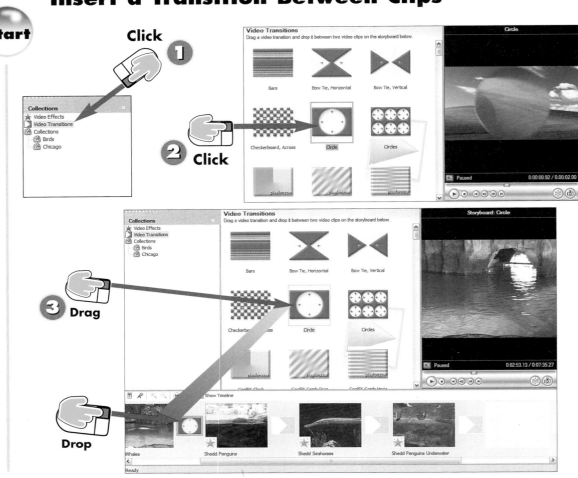

Start

Click ①

② **Click**

③ **Drag**

Drop

1. Open the Transitions collection by clicking on **Video Transitions**.

2. Click to select a transition in the group of available video transitions and then click **Play** in the monitor to preview it.

3. Find the transition you want to use between two clips and drag and drop it onto the Storyboard.

Rather than abruptly moving from one clip to the next, you insert a transition between clips to give the movie a more seamless appearance. Transitions take many different forms depending on the software you are using. In Movie Maker, transitions are a separate collection and can be added from either the Storyboard or the Timeline.

Use Transitions Sparingly
Watch TV and look at how professional editors use transitions. Unless you are watching music videos, you barely notice the change from one scene to the next. Keep this in mind before adding bow tie and star wipes between every clip.

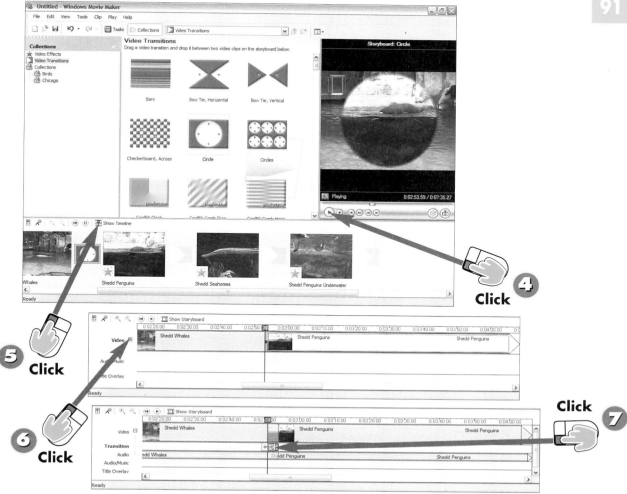

(4) Click **Play** on the monitor to preview the transition you inserted between movie clips.

(5) Click the **Show Timeline** button.

(6) Expand the video timeline by clicking the **plus sign** next to video, which reveals the transition.

(7) Select the transition by clicking on it, and then drag the left side of the transition to increase or decrease the duration as needed.

End

Finishing Up
Preview the transition after you add it and make adjustments in the Timeline as necessary. Repeat the steps to add transitions between other video clips.

Deleting Unwanted Transitions
If you decide you don't want to use a transition after adding it to the storyboard or timeline, simply highlight it and press the **Delete** key on the keyboard.

Rendering Time
Rendering is what Movie Maker does to output the completed movie to a file. While adding transitions between clips looks cool, it also increases file size, complicates the rendering process, and doesn't translate well to video compressed for viewing on the Web.

Adding Dissolves Between Clips

Start

Click ①

Drag ②

Drop

Click ③

Click ④

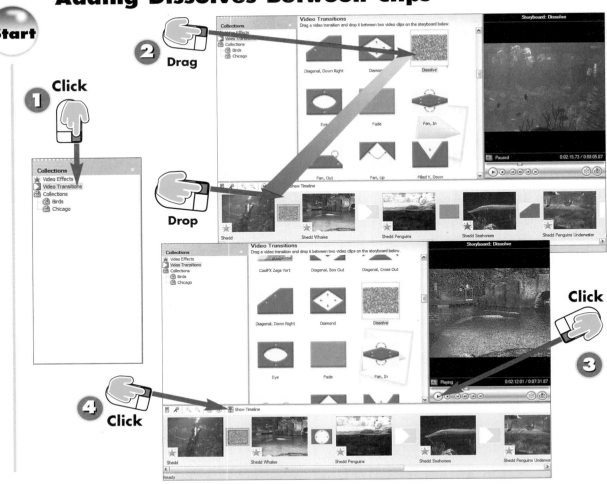

① Click **Video Transitions** in the Collections pane.

② Scroll through the list of transitions, until you find **Dissolve**, and then drag the dissolve transition between two video clips on the Storyboard or Timeline.

③ Click the **Play** button on the monitor to preview the transition.

④ If you are in Storyboard view, switch to Timeline view by clicking the **Show Timeline** button.

Dissolves are one of the most common transitions used in video production. They gradually replace the current scene with the next scene by fading in pieces of the new scene as the old scene disappears.

HINT

Directional Dissolves
Pixelan's SpiceFX Pack 1 includes several directional dissolves, which function like a regular dissolve and start at one side of the screen, gradually dissolving the picture across the screen until reaching the other side.

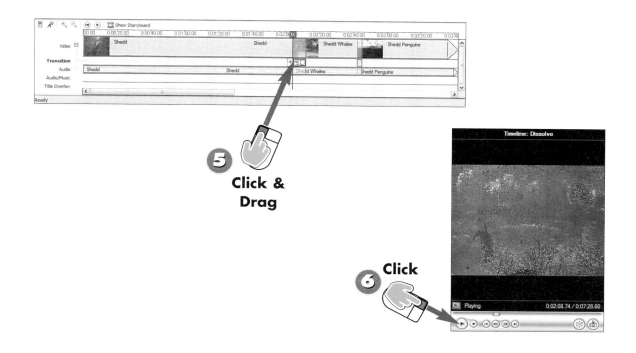

5 Click &
Drag

Click

5 Adjust the length of the dissolve as necessary by dragging the left edge of the dissolve.

6 Click **Play** on the monitor to preview the changes.

End

Movie Maker Memory
If you expanded the Timeline at any point during the editing process, Movie Maker remembers this and the Timeline remains expanded even after switching the view back to Storyboard.

Moving the Story Along
When there are abrupt changes in the movie, like a sudden shift in a person's location in a room, or passage of time, dissolves are typically used to show a shift in perspective without causing the viewer to feel like they missed something.

Adding Fades Between Clips

Start

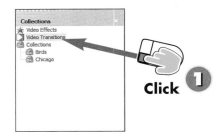

Click ①

② **Drag**

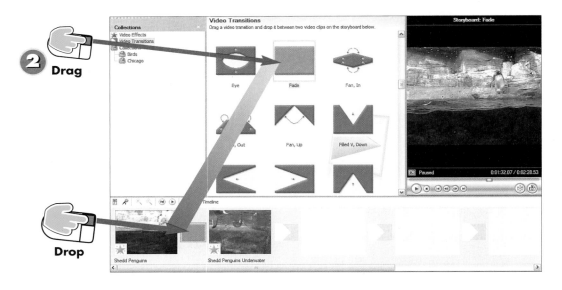

Drop

① Click **Video Transitions** in the Collections pane.

② Scroll through the list of transitions, until you find **Fade**, and then drag and drop the **Fade** transition between two video clips on the Storyboard or Timeline.

More subtle than a dissolve is the fade transition. This smooth transition between scenes is one of the cleanest ways to change scenes or introduce new clips.

HINT

Only One Transition
Movie Maker supports the use of only one transition between two movie clips. You can't dissolve into a different transition.

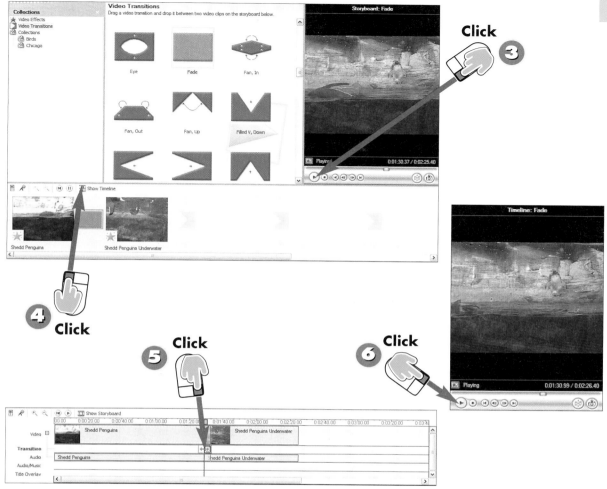

3 Click **Play** on the monitor to preview the fade transition.

4 If you are in Storyboard view, switch to Timeline view by clicking the **Show Timeline** button.

5 Adjust the length of the fade as necessary by dragging the left edge of the fade.

6 Click **Play** on the monitor to preview the changes.

End

Transition Duration
Movie Maker sets the default duration of a transition to 1.25 seconds. In most instances, this is long enough as is.

Cross Fading
The type of fade described here is known as a cross fade, which is a less-abrupt dissolve of one scene into the next. This is not to be confused with a Fade In or Fade Out which takes the scene from or to black respectively.

Adding Titles to the Beginning of the Movie

Start

Click

1

2 **Click**

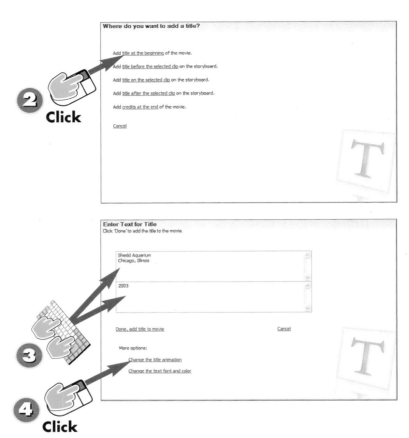

Where do you want to add a title?

Add title at the beginning of the movie.

Add title before the selected clip on the storyboard.

Add title on the selected clip on the storyboard.

Add title after the selected clip on the storyboard.

Add credits at the end of the movie.

Cancel

Enter Text for Title
Click 'Done' to add the title to the movie.

Shedd Aquarium
Chicago, Illinois

2003

Done, add title to movie   Cancel

More options:
    Change the title animation
    Change the text font and color

3

4 **Click**

1 Open the Titles pane from the menu by selecting **Tools**, **Titles and Credits**.

2 Click **Add title at the beginning of the movie**.

3 Type the main text for the title in the top text box. Subtext may be included in the bottom box.

4 Click **Change the title animation** to modify the way Movie Maker presents the opening credit text.

Titles at the beginning of a movie generally consist of opening credits and can also be used to preface a movie with information about what the viewer will see.

Not Just a Title

The opening title slide can be more than just the title of your movie. Include background information like the name of the city, time of day, and any other details to help set the stage for onscreen events.

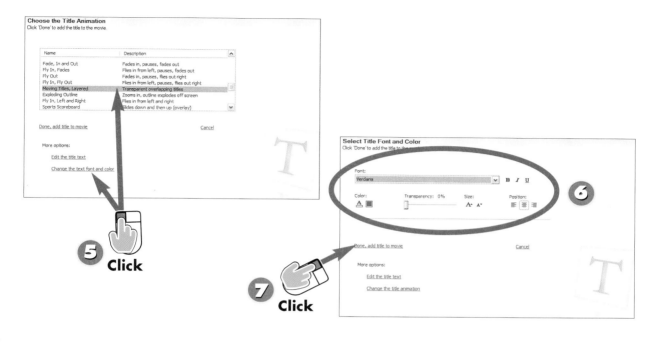

5 Select a new animation style, if desired, and then click **Change the text font and color**.

6 Modify text attributes like background color, font, text color, and positioning by making selections at the top of the dialog box.

7 Finish the opening title by clicking **Done, add title to movie**.

8 The title is now located at the beginning of the storyboard.

End

Adding Multiple Titles
Add additional title screens to the beginning of your movie for more complex opening credits. This offers you the chance to feature information about the director and featured members of the movie using a sequence of screens rather than trying to fit all information on one title segment.

Title Transitions
Transitions may be inserted between a title and a movie clip, just like any other two segments of your project.

Adding a Title Between Movie Clips

Start

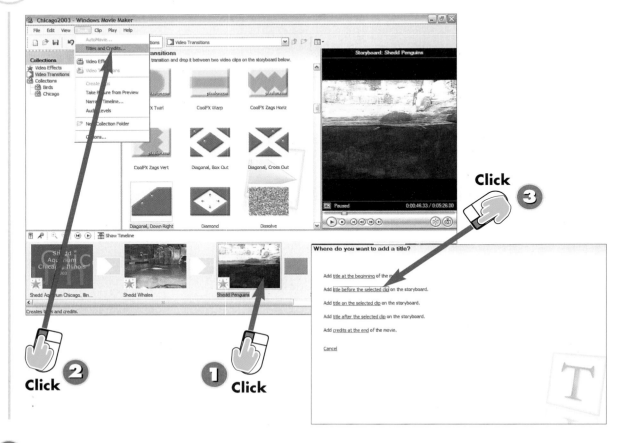

Click ③

Click ②

① **Click**

① Click the movie clip on the storyboard that requires a lead-in title.

② Choose **Tools, Titles and Credits** from the Menu.

③ Click **Add title before the selected clip on the storyboard**.

Insert titles between movie clips to provide a quick way to explain passage of time or abrupt scene changes. Titles can make great substitutes for transitions between clips.

INFO

Subtitles

Movie Maker also includes a subtitles title option that allows you to place text on top of the video at the bottom of the screen.

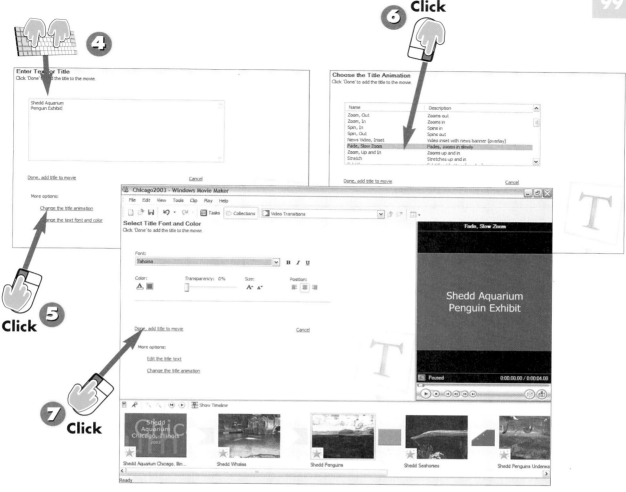

4 Type the text for the title slide.

5 Click **Change the title animation**.

6 Select the animation for the title text and then click **Change the text font and color**.

7 You can change the text formatting options at the top of the window. Click **Done, add title to movie** when finished.

Long Text Gets Cut Off
Title animations, like Newspaper and Sports Scoreboards, are prone to having long text cut off. Aside from abbreviating your title text, using small font sizes and fonts with narrow spacing between letters will help prevent text cutoff.

Choose Title Fonts with Care
It's tempting to use fancy text styles for titles. The more complex a font is, the harder it will be to read it on the TV screen or in a tiny video created for the Web.

Adding a Title to a Movie Clip

Start

Click ③

Click ②

Click ①

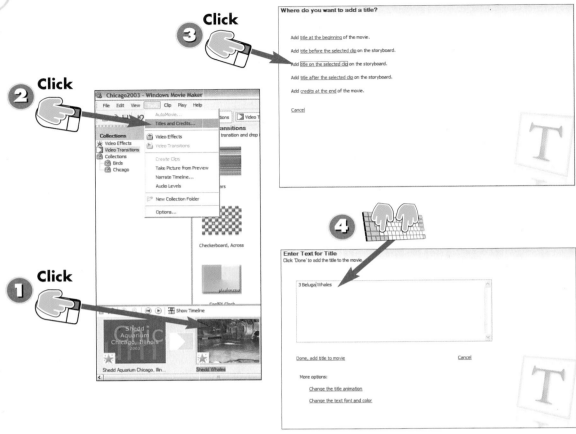

Where do you want to add a title?

Add title at the beginning of the movie.

Add title before the selected clip on the storyboard.

Add title on the selected clip on the storyboard.

Add title after the selected clip on the storyboard.

Add credits at the end of the movie.

Cancel

④

Enter Text for Title
Click 'Done' to add the title to the movie.

3 Beluga Whales

Done, add title to movie   Cancel

More options:

Change the title animation

Change the text font and color

---

1 Click the movie clip you will be adding a title to in the storyboard.

2 Choose **Tools**, **Titles and Credits** from the Menu.

3 Click **Add title on the selected clip on the storyboard**.

4 Type the text for the title slide.

Adding titles directly to a movie clip is a great way to label footage for the reader, convey date information, or present other statistics.

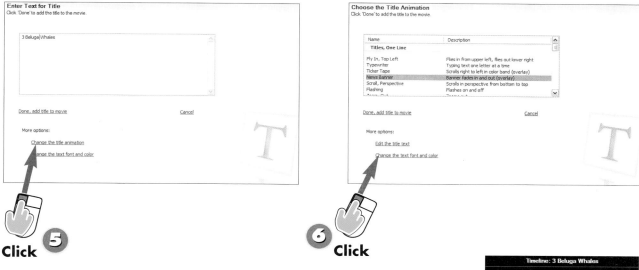

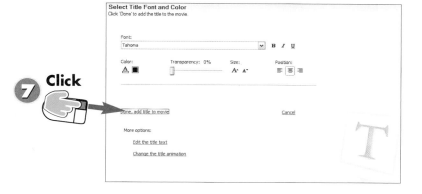

5 Click **Change the title animation**.

6 Select the animation for the title text. Click **Change the text font and color** when you are finished.

7 Choose the text attributes you want to modify from the options at the top of the window. Click **Done, add title to movie** when you finish.

Overlay Titles Added in Timeline View
Overlay titles display over the top of a movie image. Movie Maker includes Ticker Tape and News Banner overlays, in addition to subtitling. If you add a title with the "(overlay)" designation after it, Movie Maker will warn you it needs to switch to Timeline view to insert the title. Title overlays appear as a separate item on the video timeline.

Titles Over Stills
Title overlays can also be added on top of still photos, giving your titles a more colorful background.

Adding Credits to Your Movie

Start

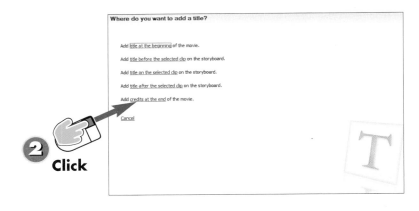

1 **Click**

AutoMovie...
Titles and Credits...
Video Effects
Video Transitions
Create Clips
Take Picture from Preview
Narrate Timeline...
Audio Levels
New Collection Folder
Options...

Where do you want to add a title?

Add title at the beginning of the movie.

Add title before the selected clip on the storyboard.

Add title on the selected clip on the storyboard.

Add title after the selected clip on the storyboard.

Add credits at the end of the movie.

Cancel

2 **Click**

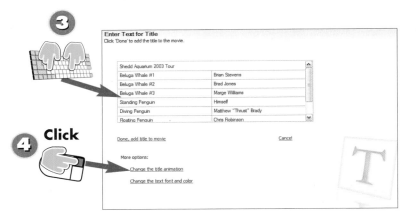

3

Enter Text for Title
Click 'Done' to add the title to the movie.

Shedd Aquarium 2003 Tour	
Beluga Whale #1	Brian Stevens
Beluga Whale #2	Brad Jones
Beluga Whale #3	Marge Williams
Standing Penguin	Himself
Diving Penguin	Matthew "Thrust" Brady
Floating Penguin	Chris Robinson

Done, add title to movie   Cancel

More options:

Change the title animation

Change the text font and color

4 **Click**

1 Open the title pane by choosing **Tools**, **Titles and Credits** from the menu.

2 Click **Add credits at the end of the movie**.

3 Type the credits title text and cast and crew information.

4 Click **Change the title animation**.

Generations of movie-goers are familiar with the scrolling list of who did what immediately following the final scene of a movie. Movie Maker includes several credit effects for listing the cast and crew of your production.

HINT

Credits Soundtrack
Add a music soundtrack to the credits from Timeline view, just like adding audio to your movie (see Part 8). Reprise the movie's theme song while the credits roll or select credit-specific music.

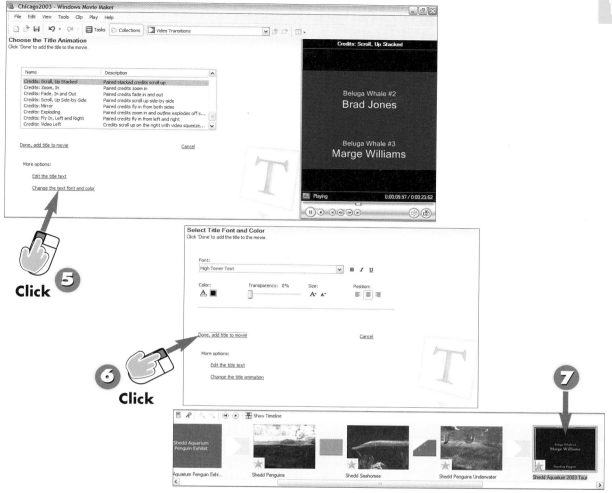

Click **5**

Click **6**

7

5 Choose the animation for your title text and then click **Change the text font and color** when you are finished.

6 Make any text adjustments, and then click **Done, add title to movie** when you finish making text changes.

7 Verify the credits now appear at the end of your movie in the storyboard.

End

Multiple Credit Styles
To use multiple credit animation styles, create part of the credits in one style, and then click **Done, add title to movie**. Create a second credit clip containing the additional credits using the other animation style.

Credit Overlays
The **Credits:Video Left** and **Credits:Video Top** animations are designed to show credits on top of a movie clip. Create your own "deleted scenes" reel, or just surprise viewers with extra footage during the credits.

Creating Custom Titles in Microsoft Paint

Start

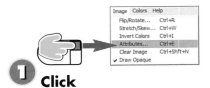

1 Click

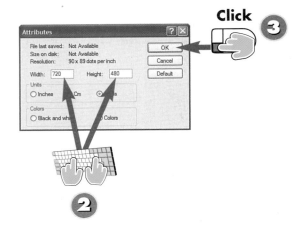

Click 3

2

1. Open Microsoft Paint by choosing **Start**, **All Programs**, **Accessories**, **Paint**. From the menu choose **Image**, **Attributes**.

2. Type **720** in the Width box and **480** in the Height box, which represents standard digital video resolution.

3. Verify **Pixels** is selected in the **Units** section and **Colors** is selected in the **Colors** section. Click **OK** when finished.

When the titles bundled in Movie Maker don't meet your needs, create your own using Microsoft Paint, an imaging application included with Windows.

Paint Remembers
The next time you open Paint, 720x480 will be the default size because it remembers the most recently used work area configuration.

104

PART 7

Click **4**

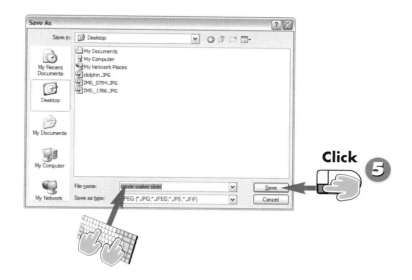

Click **5**

4 Choose **File**, **Save As**.

5 Type a name for your file and click **Save** to save your work area using the default JPEG setting.

See next page

Other File Formats
Paint also saves images as .bmp, .gif, .tiff, and .png format files.

HINT

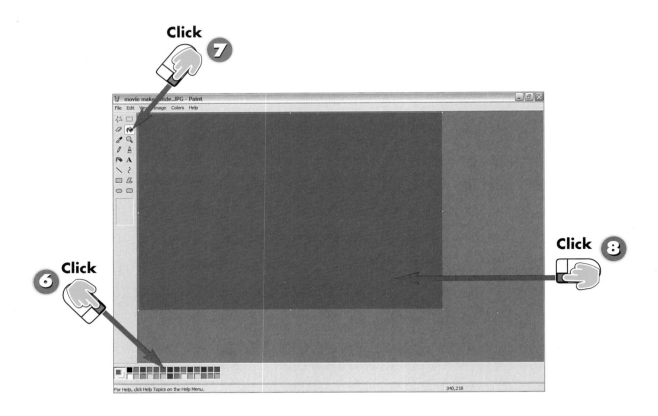

Click ⑦

Click ⑧

⑥ **Click**

⑥ Change the background color of the slide by choosing a color from the Color Box at the bottom of the screen.

⑦ Select the **Fill with Color** tool from the **Tool Box** by clicking it.

⑧ Click on the work area to change the background color.

Once the basic work area is prepared, it's time to start the fun part—making a title slide.

TIP

Multicolored Backgrounds
Create a background with several colors by using the **Select** tool in Paint, choosing a new color, and then coloring the selected area using the **Fill with Color** tool.

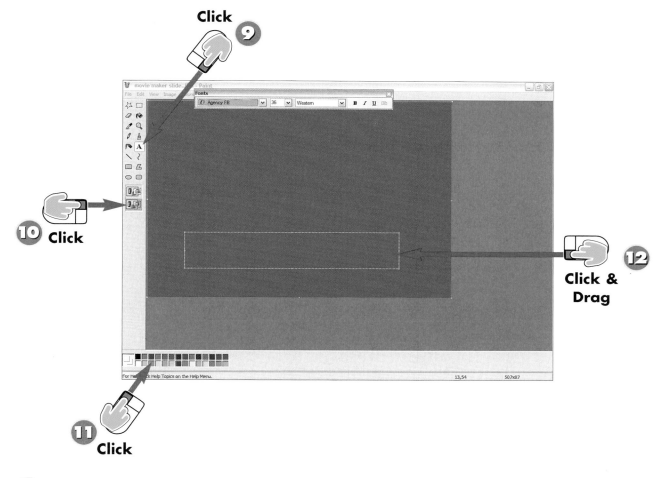

Click 9

10 **Click**

11 **Click**

12 **Click & Drag**

9 Select the **Text** tool by clicking it.

10 Select the **Transparent text box** option.

11 Choose a text color from the **Color Box**.

12 Draw a text box on the work area by clicking and dragging the mouse.

 See next page

Text Box Background

TIP To create a text box with a white background, choose the **Solid text box** option, and then select the text color from the color box.

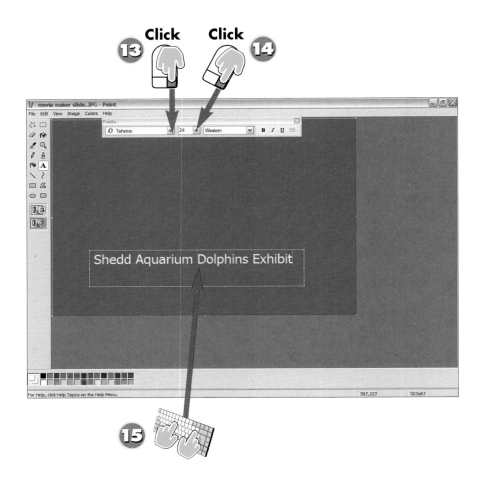

Click **Click**

13 Choose a font from the drop-down menu.

14 Select the font size for your text from the drop-down with numbers, and select any text attributes.

15 Type your title text in the text box.

After laying out the background, add text and image elements to your title slide.

Multiple Fonts

Paint only allows one font in a text box. To create text using more than one font, type text in the first font, and then create a second text box for the remaining text in the additional font.

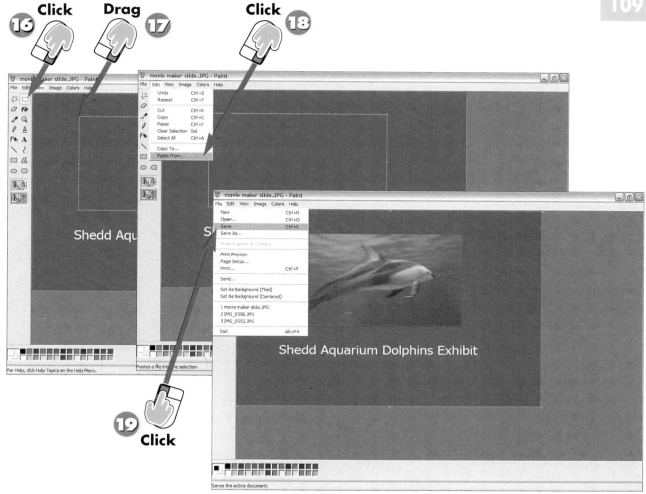

16 Click the **Select** tool to create an image box.

17 With the left mouse button pressed, drag the mouse on the work area until you get a box sized to fit your image.

18 Click **Paste From** on the **Edit** menu, and then select the image you want to insert.

19 Save your slide again by choosing **File**, **Save** from the menu. Close Microsoft Paint when you are finished.

Text Toolbar
If the Text Toolbar isn't visible, select **View**, **Text Toolbar** from the menu.

TV Safe Area
If you plan on outputting your movie for viewing on a television screen, don't start text and images at the very edge of the slide. Leave some empty space around the edge of your title slide. TVs overscan projected images by as much as 10% of the image, which means some portion of the image is actually showing off screen.

Creating Title Slides with PowerPoint

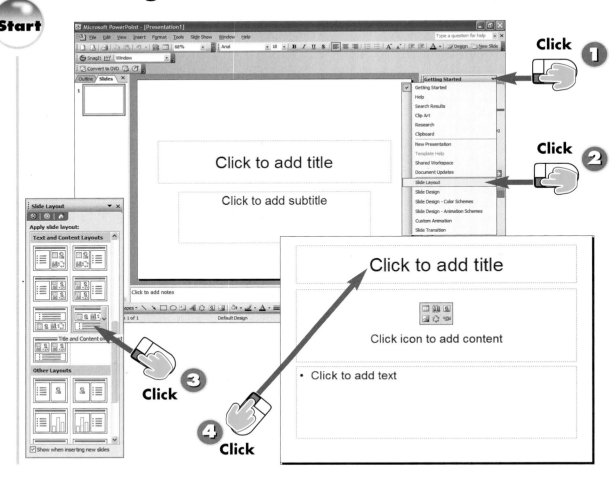

1 Open the PowerPoint application, and then click the arrow next to **Getting Started** on the **Task Pane**.

2 Choose **Slide Layout** from the drop-down menu.

3 Select a **Slide Layout** from the available options. In this case, we are choosing **Title and Content over Text**.

4 Click the area labeled **Click to add title** and type the title information for the slide.

Microsoft PowerPoint is one of the easiest tools to use for creating Movie Maker titles. PowerPoint provides control over text placement, allows users to add custom background designs, and supports inserting images on slides. Exporting a single PowerPoint slide as an image, which is the method used when saving slides for titling, is a standard feature.

I Don't See the Task Pane
If the Getting Started task pane isn't visible when you open PowerPoint, you can access the Slide Layout task pane by selecting **Format**, **Slide Layout**.

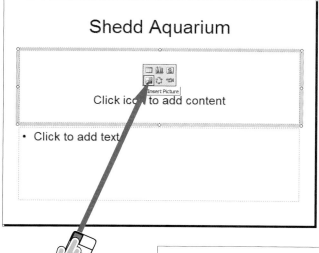

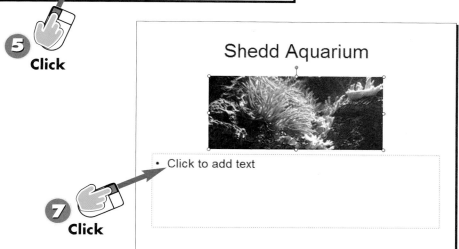

5 **Click**

6 **Click**

7 **Click**

5 Click the **Insert Picture** button in the content section of the slide.

6 Choose a picture to include on the slide and click the **Insert** button.

7 Click the **Click to add text** item in the bottom section of the slide and type additional text on the slide.

See next page

Incompatible Features
Movie Maker requires
PowerPoint slides to be saved
as image files, like .JPG, .GIF,
or .PNG, so you cannot include
any animated text or movies on
the title slides created in
PowerPoint.

More PowerPoint Layouts
Microsoft frequently updates the
library of available Slide Layouts
and Slide Designs with additional
content in the template gallery
at Microsoft Office Online
(http://office.microsoft.com).

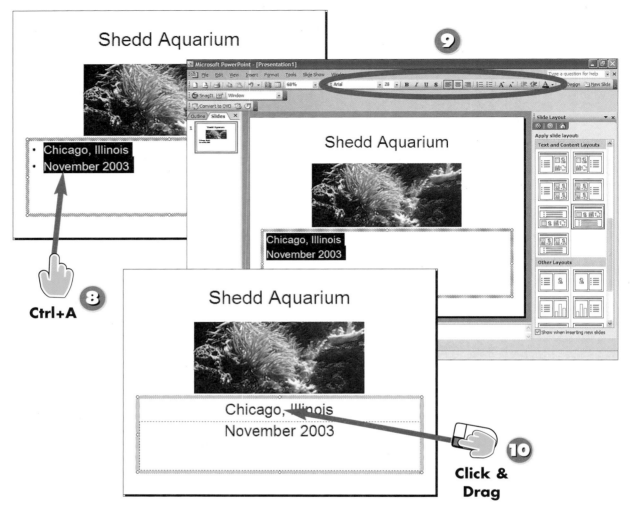

Ctrl+A

Click & Drag

8 Select all the text in the bottom text area by pressing **Ctrl+A** on the keyboard.

9 Make any desired changes to the default text formatting using the buttons on the Formatting toolbar.

10 Adjust the size of the bottom text area by clicking the circle in the top center of the textbox and dragging it toward the bottom of the slide.

After creating a basic layout using a predefined Slide Layout, further customization of the slide is possible. Modifying text attributes, adding backgrounds, and adjusting the position of elements on the slide allows you to fully maximize the versatility of using PowerPoint to create slides.

Moving Text Boxes

If PowerPoint doesn't put text boxes where you want them on the slide, hover over the text box with the mouse pointer until it turns into a plus-sign with arrows pointing in all directions. Click and hold the mouse button as you move the text box to a new position on the screen.

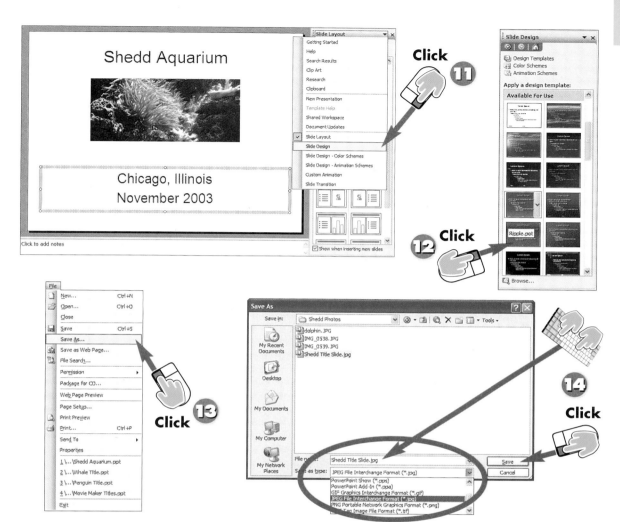

Click **11**

Click **12**

Click **13**

Click **14**

11 Click the arrow next to Slide Layout on the task pane and choose **Slide Design** from the drop-down menu.

12 Select a background design from the list of options by clicking one of the designs in the **Available for Use** list.

13 Choose **File**, **Save As** from the menu (or press the F12 key on the keyboard).

14 Select the location to save your slide, name the file, choose **JPEG File Interchange Format (*.jpg)** from the **Save as type** options, and then click the **Save** button.

End

Custom Backgrounds
To use your own image as the background for a slide, select **Format**, **Background**. In the list of background options, choose **Fill Effects** and click the **Picture** tab to add your own image file.

Changing Text Color
When using one of the background designs from the PowerPoint Design Layout, the text color on your slides changes to match the defaults for the Design Layout you choose. To switch the text color, first select the text on the slide, and then choose a new color from the dropdown text color button on the Formatting toolbar.

Adding Custom Titles to the Movie

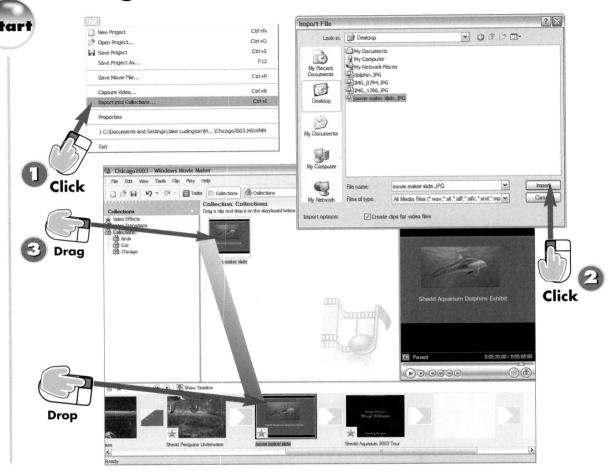

1 Choose **File**, **Import into Collections**.

2 Choose your custom title slide and click the **Import** button.

3 Drag the title from the collections pane to the point on the storyboard where you want to insert the title.

Adding Effects to Movie Clips

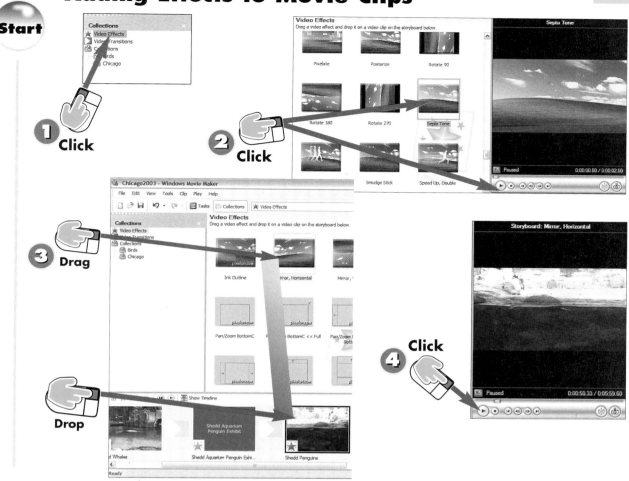

Start

1 **Click**

2 **Click**

3 **Drag**

Drop

4 **Click**

1 Click **Video Effects** in the Collections pane at the left side of your screen.

2 Click an effect in the group of available video effects and then click **Play** in the monitor to preview the effect.

3 Find the effect you want to use and drag and drop it to the movie clip on which you want to use the effect.

4 Click **Play** on the monitor to preview the movie clip and effect.

End

INTRODUCTION

Video effects enhance movie clips by adding artistic or color correcting tweaks to the video file. Movie Maker's available effects are stored in the Video Effects collection.

TIP

Multiple Effects
Layer multiple video effects on the same video clip to create custom effects for your movie.

HINT

For some effects, trying them out on a video clip provides a better preview. Notice that the star on the clip will turn blue, which signifies a clip with an effect.

Converting Your Movie to Black and White

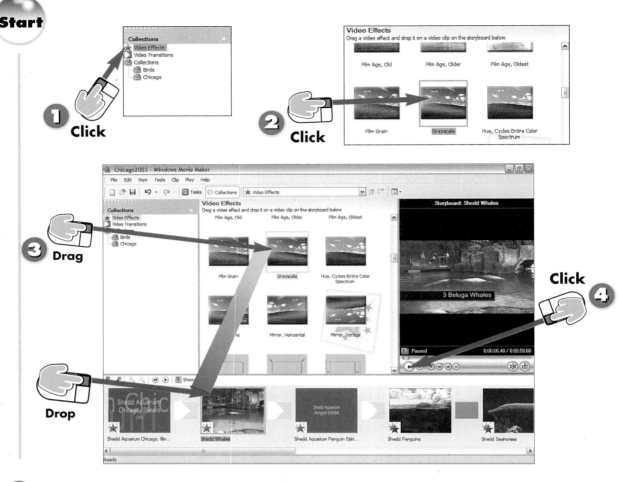

Start

1 Click

2 Click

3 Drag

Drop

Click 4

1. Click **Video Effects** in the Collections pane at the left side of your screen.

2. Scroll through the list of effects and select **Grayscale**.

3. Drag and drop the **Grayscale** effect onto each movie clip in the Storyboard that you want to appear in black and white. Movie Maker won't show the grayscale effect on the Storyboard; it only appears in the monitor during preview.

4. Click **Play** on the monitor to preview the movie clip and effect.

End

One of the more commonly used video effects is to convert color footage to black and white. In Movie Maker, the Grayscale effect is used to achieve black-and-white footage.

TIP

Sepia Tone
Give your movie an antique tin-type photo appearance with this brown-and-white effect. Anywhere that you see shades of gray in the Grayscale effect, you would see degrees of brown in Sepia Tone.

Enhancing the Brightness of the Movie

Start

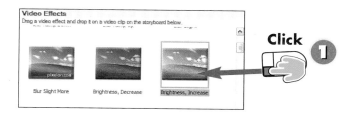

Click ❶

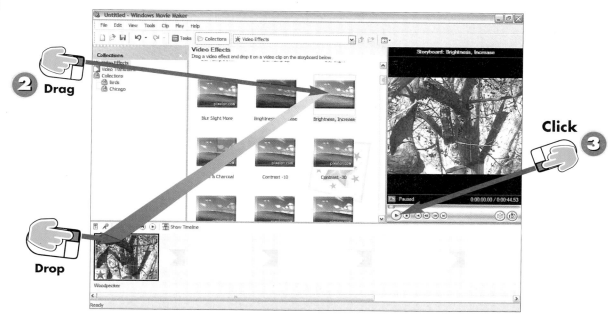

❷ Drag

Drop

Click ❸

❶ With Video Effects selected in the collections pane, click **Brightness**, **Increase** to increase brightness (or Brightness, Decrease to reduce the brightness) in the list of effects.

❷ Drag and drop the **Brightness**, **Increase** effect onto the movie clip in the Storyboard that you want to enhance.

❸ Click **Play** on the monitor to preview the movie clip and effect.

End

If some of the colors in your video are either too bright or too washed out, the Brightness effects may offer a corrective fix. However, keep in mind that software effects are never a real substitute for good lighting when the video is originally shot.

Use Brightness Sparingly
Minor adjustments to brightness or contrast can help improve some footage. Too much of either will introduce video noise, making the footage look pixelated.

Maximizing Effects
Each effect may be added to the same clip up to six times in order to maximize the effect.

Adjusting Contrast with Pixelan Effects

Start

Click ①

Drag ②

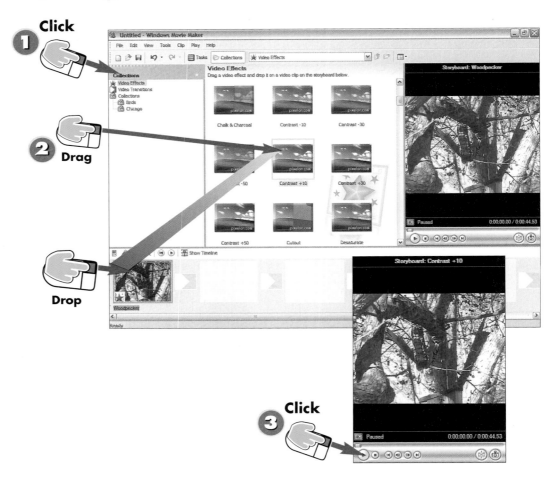

Drop

Click ③

① Click **Video Effects** in the collections pane.

② Drag and drop an effect onto a clip in the Storyboard. The sample clip needs the Woodpecker's black color to be more distinguishable from the shadow, so Contrast +10 is the effect being used.

③ Click **Play** on the monitor to preview the movie clip and effect.

End

Six contrast effects for Movie Maker are available in the Pixelan SpiceFX packs. Contrast adjustment modifies the depth of gray and black tones in movie clips by lighting the highlights in an image and darkening the shadows. The result brings more definition to the image when used in moderation.

TIP

Try Again
If the contrast adjustment was not sufficient, replace it with the next greater effect (in this case Contrast Increase +30) and repeat.

HINT

Clipping a Clip
If only a small portion of a movie clip has a contrast problem, divide the clip into smaller clips, isolating the trouble spot. This allows you to retain the original coloration for most of the clip, while applying the effect only to the area it is needed.

Applying Color Correction with Pixelan Effects

Start

Click ①

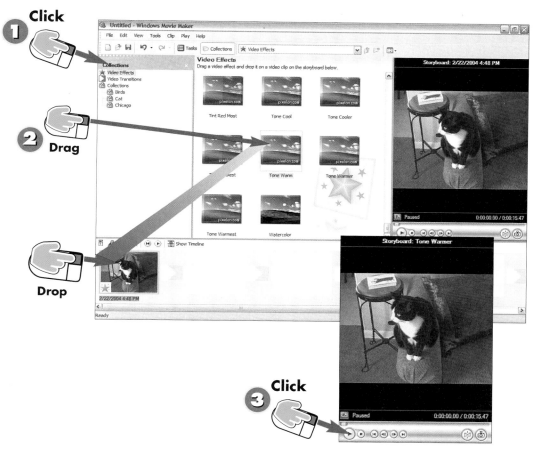

Drag ②

Drop

Click ③

① Click **Video Effects** in the collections pane.

② Drag and drop a tone effect onto a clip in the Storyboard. In the example, the video has a slightly blue cast to it, so adding a warmer tone should make it look more natural.

③ Click **Play** on the monitor to preview the movie clip and effect. In this case, the picture still has a slightly blue cast, so Tone Warm will be replaced with Tone Warmer.

End

INTRODUCTION
SpiceFX includes six color correction effects for adjusting footage that is either too warm (has a reddish cast) or too cool (has a blue cast). The Tone Cooler effects add varying levels of blue tint to the image, while Tone Warmer effects add red tints.

HINT
Applying Tint
Pixelan also includes 12 tint settings designed to increase a specific color in the video clip. These can be used for color correction or for setting a particular mood within the movie.

Adding Audio to Your Video

The audio associated with a movie is just as important as the video. In some cases audio is even more important. Audio can consist of the actual sounds or dialog occurring when the video was created. Soundtrack music can be used to enhance the emotions associated with your video. If a description of events transpiring in the movie makes sense, adding a narrative track will improve the experience of your viewers.

Windows Movie Maker, in combination with Windows Media Player, allows you to add soundtrack files to your movie. Using an external audio editing application, it's possible to level the sound of all the songs in the soundtrack using a process known as normalization. Narration is accomplished easily within the Movie Maker application by viewing the movie and talking into a microphone as you watch.

In addition to adding soundtrack audio and narration, Movie Maker allows you to perform custom edits on the audio tied to your movie clips. J-cuts and L-cuts are two audio edits which act as transitions between scenes. Making minor adjustments to the volume of the original audio file is also possible. In this part of the book, you will learn how to edit and improve the audio for your video.

Audio Editing on the Movie Maker Timeline

Add music to
your movie

Adjust the
Audio Levels

Add Narration
to your movie

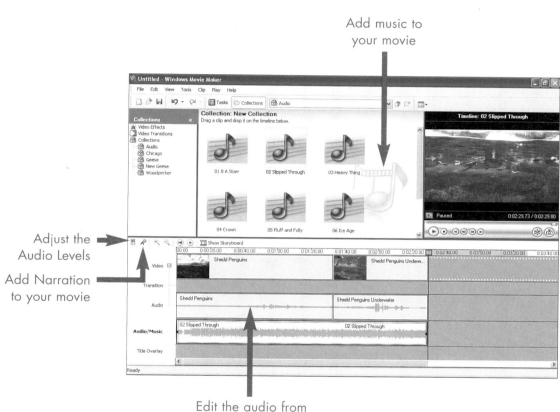

Edit the audio from
the video clips

Narrating a Video

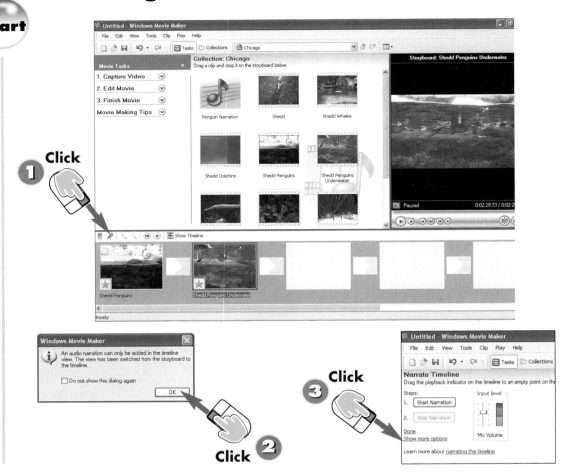

Start

Click 1

Click 2

Click 3

1. With your movie project open, click the microphone icon on the **Storyboard** or **Timeline** toolbar.

2. If Movie Maker is in Storyboard view, click **OK** on the dialog box informing you of the switch to Timeline view.

3. Click the **Show more options** link.

Narrating is as easy as talking about what you see in the video as it happens. Movie Maker provides an interface to all the necessary components of Windows for narrating audio.

Quiet on the Set
Make sure the room is quiet during narration. Close the door and send kids or co-workers out of the room. Computer microphones pick up background noise, which will be permanent in your recordings. Turn off the phones.

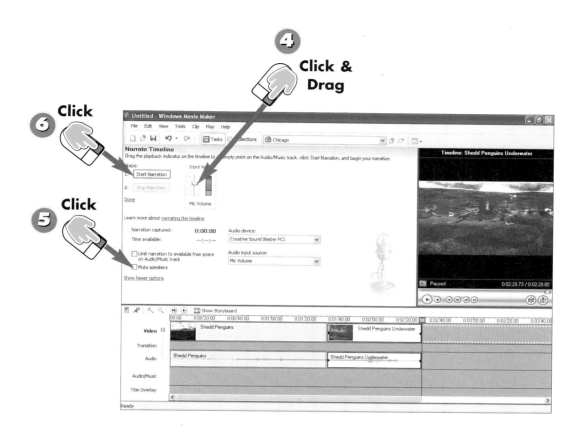

4 Click and drag the slider on the **Input level** so the Mic volume is somewhere below the red zone near the top.

5 Click the **Mute speakers** button to eliminate echo during recording.

6 Click **Start Narration**, begin talking, and then click **Stop Narration** when you finish talking.

 See next page

Monitoring Narration

TIP

If you need to hear yourself as you are recording, use headphones as the speakers for the computer during the narration process. This eliminates the risk of echo caused by external speakers, while allowing you to hear the audio.

Headset Microphones

TIP

To get even better narrative audio, try using a headset microphone. Headsets often combine both earphones and microphones in one unit and position the microphone near your mouth for more consistent audio levels.

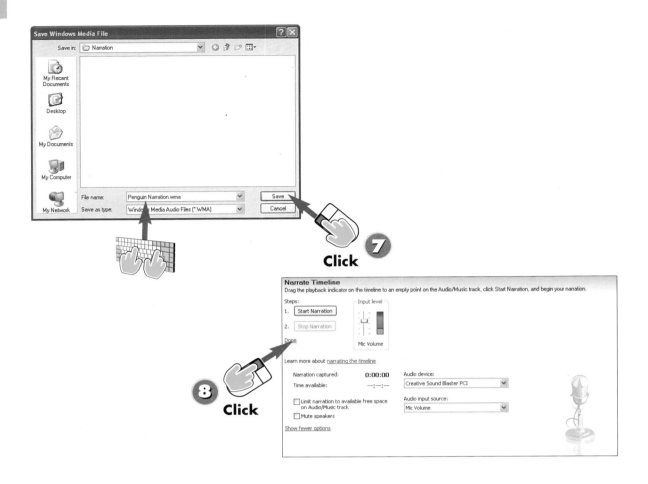

Click

Click

⑦ Choose a file name and click **Save**.

⑧ Click the **Done** link to return to the Movie Tasks pane.

End

Following the Picture
Movie Maker plays the movie in the preview monitor as you record the narration, making it easy to follow along with the action onscreen.

Dress Rehearsal
It's a good idea to run through the movie a few times to practice what you will say before recording. Lots of "ums" and "ahhs" distract from what the message of the narrative is.

Adjusting Audio Volume

Start

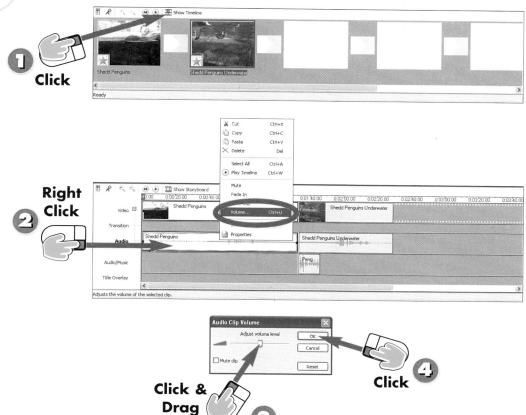

① Click

② Right Click

③ Click & Drag

④ Click

---

① Click the **Show Timeline** button, if Storyboard view is the current view.

② Right-click on an audio track in the Timeline and choose **Volume** from the menu.

③ Click and drag the volume control to the desired audio level.

④ Click **OK**.

End

The audio volume controls how loud or quiet each individual movie clip will be. Adjusting volume levels is used to add emphasis to certain types of audio, while reducing the importance of other types of audio.

TIP

Muting an audio clip
Mute an entire audio clip by selecting **Mute** from the right-click menu. Muting an audio clip is useful if you are replacing the original audio clip with a soundtrack, narration, or other outside audio.

Setting Audio Levels

Start

Click

1

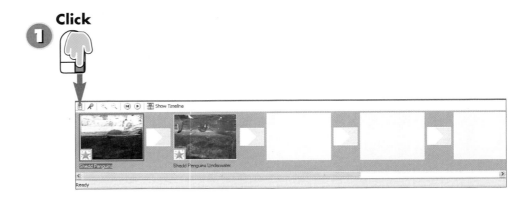

Click **3**

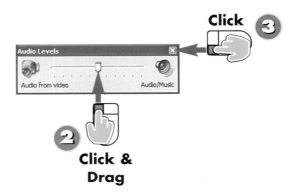

2

Click & Drag

1 Click the **Set Audio Levels** button at the far left of the Storyboard toolbar.

2 Click and drag the audio slider toward the type of audio you want to focus on in your video.

3 Close the Audio Levels window by clicking the **close** window button (the X).

End

Audio levels determine whether more focus is on the original audio from movie clips, on music and narrations, or if there is an equal balance between movie audio and soundtrack audio. The audio leveling in Movie Maker works just like the front-to-rear fade in a car. You either have a state of balance (the middle of the fader), where the audio is equally distributed between front and rear, or you have the audio skewed one direction or the other.

TIP

Audio control
For greater control over individual sections of audio, leave **Audio Levels** set to the middle. Balance between audio from video clips and soundtrack is maintained, allowing you to adjust the volume of individual clips more easily.

Adding Audio Effects

Start

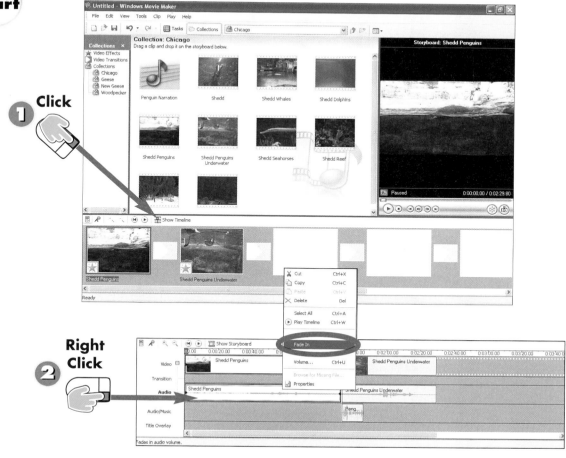

Click ①

Right Click ②

① Click **Show Timeline**, if Storyboard view is the current view.

② Right-click the audio clip you want to fade in or out and choose a fade from the menu.

End

INTRODUCTION

Fading audio in introduces viewers to an audio selection more gradually. Fading audio out makes scene changes less abrupt. Windows Movie Maker creates fades about two-thirds of a second in length.

HINT

Fading Versus Reducing Volume
When you adjust the volume of an audio clip in Movie Maker, it reduces the volume of the entire clip. Fading only affects the volume of the first or last 2/3 second of audio.

Muting Audio Tracks

Start

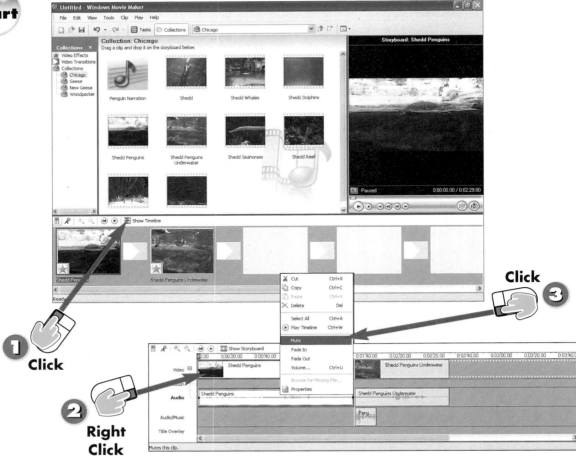

Click

Right Click

Click

1. Click **Show Timeline**, if Storyboard view is the current view.

2. **Right-click** the audio clip you want to mute.

3. Click **Mute** in the menu.

End

Windows Movie Maker allows you to mute selected audio clips. Muting a clip makes it easy to replace it with something else. This is particularly useful when the audio track of your video contains too much background noise or doesn't sound good.

TIP

Dividing Clips
If only a small portion of an audio clip needs muting, divide the clip into smaller clips to isolate the problem audio, and then mute only the small section instead of having to mute the full clip.

Extracting Music from CD with Windows Media Player

Start

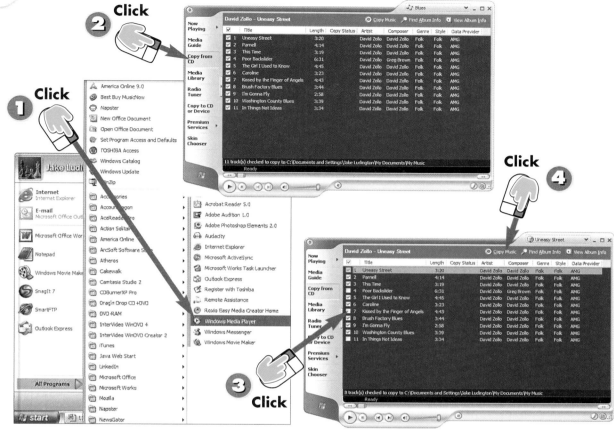

Click ② ... **Click** ① ... **Click** ④ ... **Click** ③

1 Open Windows Media Player by clicking **Start**, **All Programs**, and choosing **Windows Media Player**.

2 Insert the CD you want to copy and click **Copy from CD**.

3 Select tracks you want to copy by checking the box next to the tracks. (All tracks are selected by default.)

4 Click the **Copy Music** button.

End

INTRODUCTION

Creating a soundtrack for your movie requires adding additional music tracks. One source for music is your CD collection.

TIP

Copyright Concerns
If you plan on distributing your movie to other people, especially in cases where you might be selling it, you need to acquire permission from the copyright holders of the music before distributing the music as part of the final movie.

Importing Music in Windows Movie Maker

Start

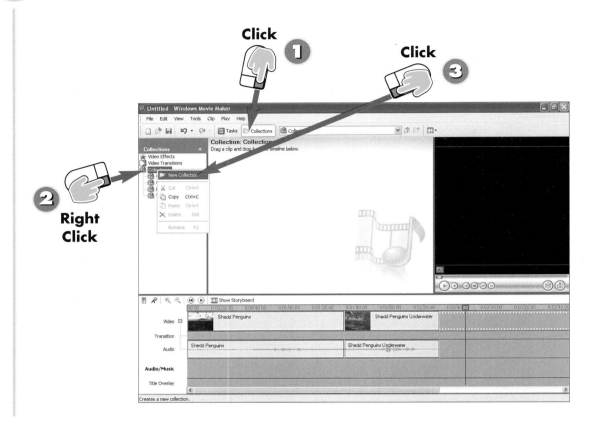

Click ①

Click ③

② Right Click

1 Click the **Collections** button on the toolbar.

2 Right-click **Collections** in the Collections Pane.

3 Choose **New Collection** from the menu.

Once music files have been copied to the hard drive, they must be imported into Movie Maker. After importing audio files into the collections, they can be added to the timeline to create a soundtrack.

Digital Rights Management
Most of the music from download sites like MusicMatch and Napster will not work in Movie Maker because it has DRM protections in place preventing the files from being re-edited in applications like Movie Maker.

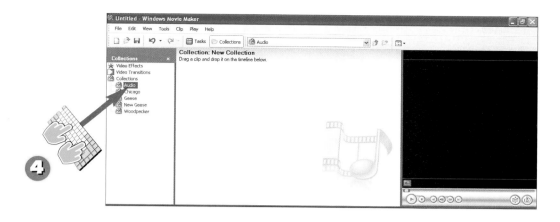

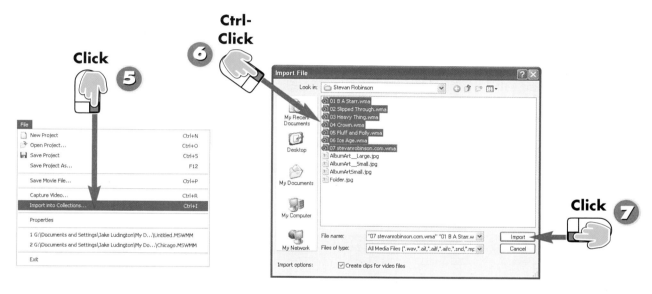

4 Type a name for the new Collection. **Audio** is a good choice.

5 Click the **File** menu and choose **Import into Collections**.

6 Ctrl-click to select the audio files for your soundtrack.

7 Click **Import**.

End

Select tracks
TIP

To import successive audio tracks from the same folder, hold down the **Shift** key and click the first track you want to select, and then click the last track. Those two tracks and all tracks between them are selected.

Adding Music to the Timeline

Start

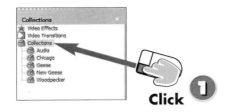

Click ①

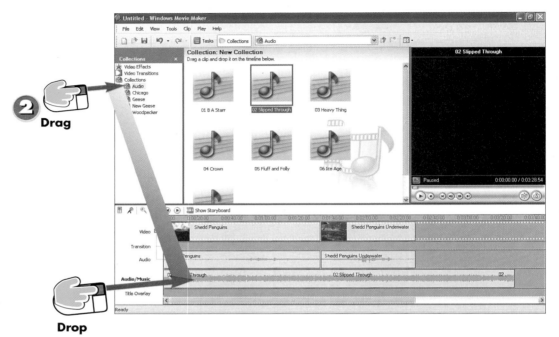

② **Drag**

Drop

① Click the collection where your audio clips are stored in the Collections pane.

② Drag the clip from the middle Collections pane and drop the track on the **Audio/Music** section of the Timeline.

End

To create a soundtrack, music tracks are added to the Timeline. The audio tracks are first inserted on the Timeline, and then positioned in the exact location where you want them to play by dragging them to a specific point in the Timeline.

Zoom the Timeline

To make placing audio clips on the Timeline easier, use the **Zoom Out** button on the timeline toolbar to expand the timeline. This allows you to position the audio at the precise instant you want it to start.

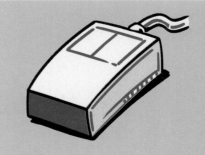

Trimming Audio Clips

Start

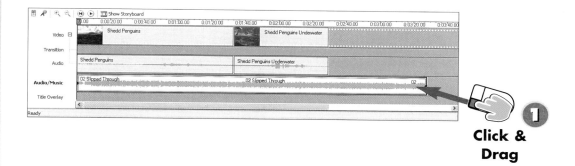

Click & Drag

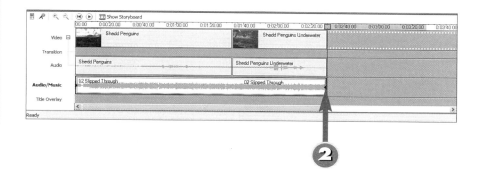

2

1 Click the end of the audio clip and drag it to the point where you want to trim it.

2 Release the mouse button when you get the clip shortened correctly.

End

When only a portion of an audio track is required for the movie, trim the audio to eliminate the part you don't need. *Trimming* involves eliminating a portion of the beginning or end of the audio file, in order to have it fit the length you need.

HINT

Eliminating Silence
Trimming audio tracks is particularly useful for eliminating extra silence at the start or end of an audio clip. Find the point where silence begins by listening to the track and making note of where the silence starts, and then adjust the track end point until you have eliminated the silence.

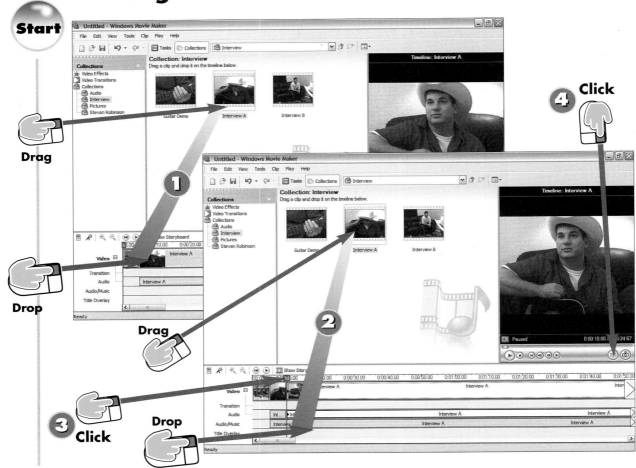

Making an Audio J-Cut

Start

Drag

Drop

Drag

3 Click

Drop

4 Click

1. Drag the two clips you want to j-cut to the **Video** section of the Timeline.

2. Drag a second copy of clip number two to the **Audio/Music** section of the timeline, lining it up with its duplicate.

3. Making sure the second video clip is selected on the timeline, click and drag the slider to the point in the second clip where you want the video to start.

4. Click the **Split Clip** button located below the monitor.

J-cut refers to an audio transition where audio from the next scene starts playing over video from the current scene. J-cuts are quite common on television, where you will often see the exterior of a building, hear a conversation happening inside the building, and then see the people having the conversation.

TIP

Nudging the Timeline
Using the **Previous Frame** and **Next Frame** buttons located below the monitor to accurately position audio and video for j-cuts will save you time and eliminate some of the frustration of trying to position the mouse exactly where you want your clip to go.

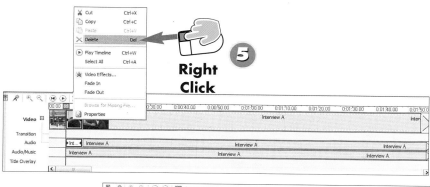

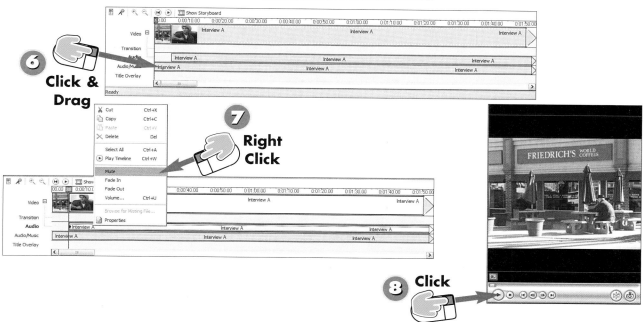

5 Right-click the newly created video clip between the first clip and the second clip and choose **Delete** from the menu.

6 Drag the audio clip on the **Audio/Music** track so it lines up with the beginning of the first video clip.

7 Right-click the audio track on the **Audio** section of the timeline and choose **Mute** from the menu.

8 Click **Play** and watch to verify the audio and video are still synchronized.

End

Combining J-Cuts and Fades

For a smoother appearance to the j-cut, add a video fade transition between the two video clips, making the scene change less abrupt.

Advanced J-Cuts

In more complex j-cuts, you may be starting the second audio track in the middle of the first track instead of at the beginning as illustrated here. Any j-cut involves simple math to determine how many seconds of the second audio track play before you reach the end of the first video track. Eliminating an equivalent number of seconds of video from the second track results in a clean j-cut.

Making an Audio L-Cut

Start

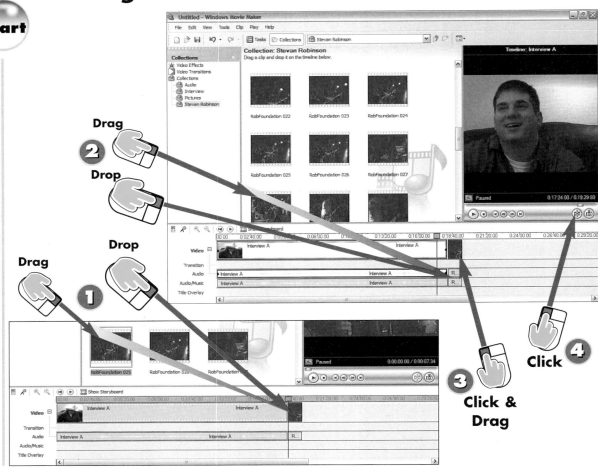

Drag
2

Drop

Drop

Drag
1

Click
4

**Click &
Drag**
3

1 Drag and drop the two clips you want to l-cut to the **Video** section of the Timeline.

2 Drag and drop a second copy of both clips to the **Audio/Music** section of the time-line, lining each up with its duplicate.

3 Making sure the first video clip is selected on the timeline, click and drag the slider to the point in the first clip where you want the second video clip to start.

4 Click the **Split Clip** button located below the monitor.

An L-Cut is the reverse of a J-Cut. The audio track from scene one keeps playing as the video from scene two is shown onscreen. This is another common television trick for filling in gaps in the plot without shooting everything.

Layering Audio
In both j-cuts and l-cuts, it's possible to overlap the audio so that both the audio that goes with the current video and the audio being cut in will play simultaneously.

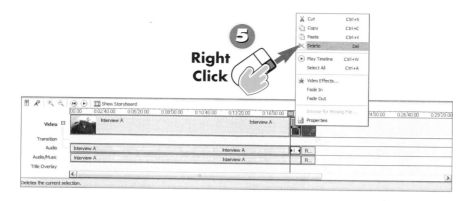

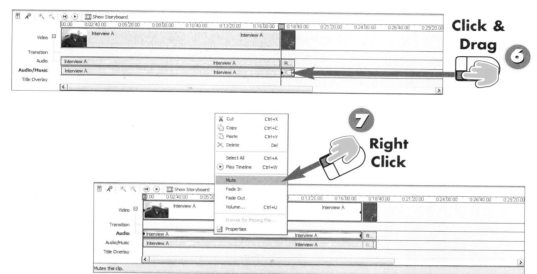

5 Right-click between the first clip and the second clip and choose **Delete**. The second video clip automatically shifts to fill in the resulting empty space.

6 Drag the second clip in the **Audio/Music** section so it lines up with the second video clip.

7 Right-click each audio track on the **Audio** section of the timeline and choose **Mute** from the menu.

End

Audio Cuts and Soundtracks
Adding custom audio transitions to the video's Audio track in addition to music for a soundtrack requires the use of an external audio editing application to combine both elements.

Filling in Gaps
L-cuts are great for filling in gaps in the story. You can keep relevant dialog from the previous scene going and lead into the next scene without having to visually illustrate how people in your movie got from point A to point B because the viewer gets to hear their course of action in the dialogue.

Preparing the Soundtrack for Normalization

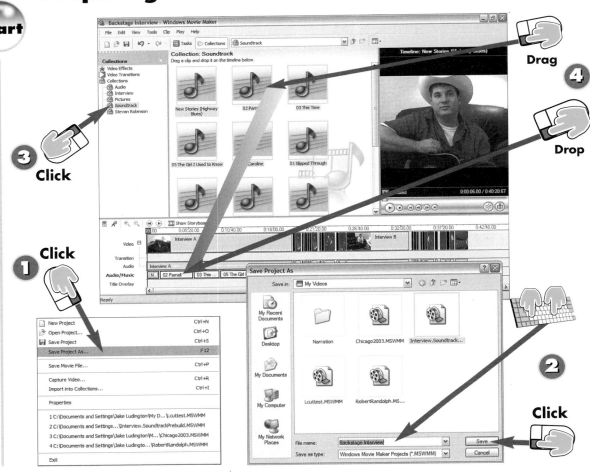

1. Choose **File, Save Project As** to save your movie project before adding the sound-track audio.

2. Name the project and click the **Save** button.

3. Click on the collection where your soundtrack clips are stored.

4. Drag the audio files for your soundtrack to the **Audio/Music** section of the timeline.

When you create a soundtrack from multiple audio sources, like songs from several different bands, the soundtrack may be very loud in some places and very quiet in others. Normalization evens out the extreme highs and lows by adjusting the volume of all tracks louder relative to the loudest point in the entire soundtrack.

External Audio Editor

Movie Maker doesn't include normalization in its audio editing feature set, so you have to perform the process in an external editor. See the next task in this part, "Normalizing Audio with Roxio Easy Media Creator."

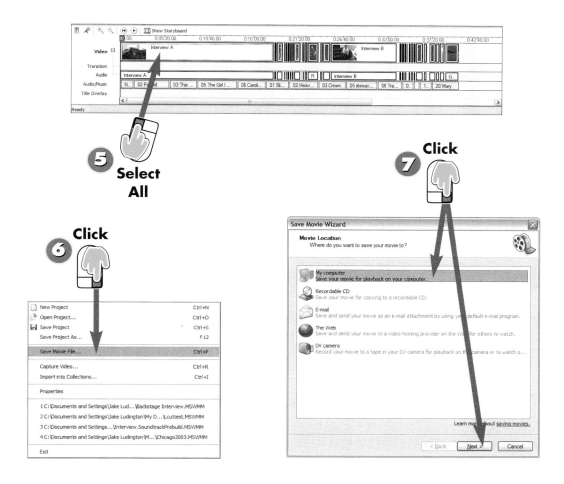

5 Click one clip in the Video section of the timeline and then press **Ctrl+A** to select all of the movie clips. Press **Delete** on your keyboard to delete the movie clips.

6 Choose **File**, **Save Movie File**.

7 Select **My Computer** from the Save Movie Wizard and click **Next**.

See next page

Save Movie Key Command

To save a Movie Maker file from the keyboard, use **Ctrl+P**. In most Windows applications this shortcut is reserved for printing, but in Movie Maker it launches the Save Movie Wizard.

Exporting Video Audio

You can also export the audio associated with a video clip by dragging the video clip to the **Audio/Music** section of the Timeline and saving the timeline as an audio file.

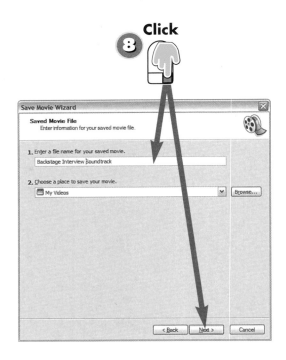

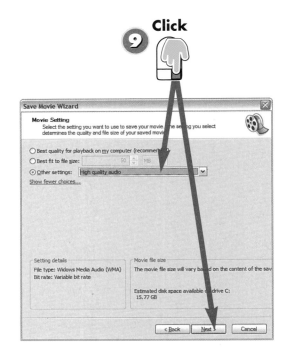

8 Type a name for the movie file, choose a folder to save the file, and then click **Next**.

9 Under **Other Settings**, choose **High quality audio**, and then click **Next**.

Although we are saving an audio file during this step, Movie Maker still refers to the file we are saving as a movie file. When you reach the point of choosing a file format, only audio formats are listed, rather than the usual list of movie formats.

Audio Quality
When you plan to edit an audio file, save it in the highest quality format available. You can always reduce the quality of the file after editing, but you can't regain quality that was removed before the editing process begins.

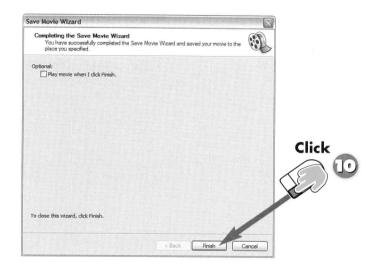

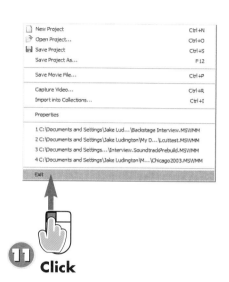

Click 10

11 **Click**

10 Click **Finish** when the audio file is done saving.

11 Close Movie Maker **without** saving the project.

End

Make Note
Make sure you document which folder the audio file is saved in. You will be opening it in another application to edit the file.

File Formats
Movie Maker saves audio files in Windows Media Audio (.wma) format. Make sure the audio editor you plan on using to edit exported audio files supports .wma audio.

Normalizing Audio with Roxio Easy Media Creator

Start

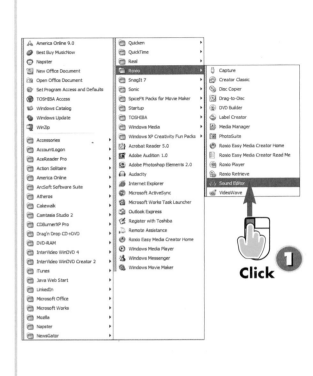

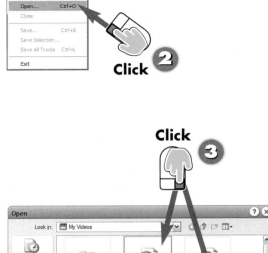

Click ②

Click ③

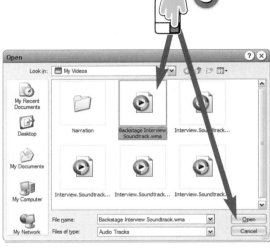

Click ①

① Open Roxio Sound Editor by clicking **Start**, **All Programs**, **Roxio**, **Sound Editor**.

② Open the audio file we created in Movie Maker by clicking **File**, **Open** in the Sound Editor menu.

③ Select the file and click **Open**.

Easy Media Creator includes a sound editor with a number of audio processing effects. By editing the soundtrack file with Easy Media Creator, you can normalize the audio, before adding it to the final Movie Maker project. Easy Media Creator is available from www.Roxio.com.

TIP

Normalizing a Portion of the Soundtrack
If you only want to edit part of the soundtrack, Sound Editor lets you click and drag anywhere in the workspace to select a segment of audio.

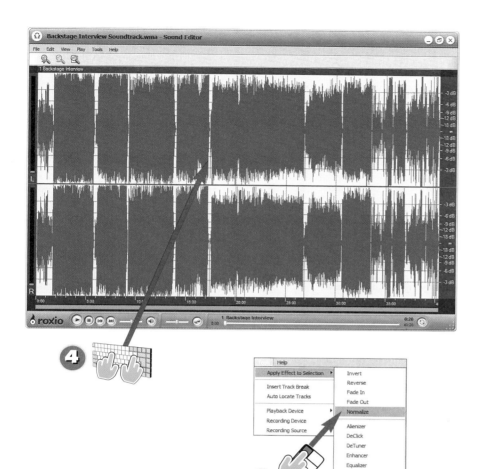

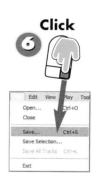

4 Select the entire soundtrack by pressing **Ctrl+A** on the keyboard.

5 From the **Tools** menu, choose **Apply Effect to Selection**, **Normalize**.

6 Click **File**, **Save**. Keep the same name as the original file, and then close Sound Editor.

End

Other Sound Editor Features

In addition to applying audio effects like Normalize, Sound Editor can import additional audio to your soundtrack, insert silence if you need it, and eliminate portions of the audio completely.

Adding the Normalized Soundtrack to Your Movie

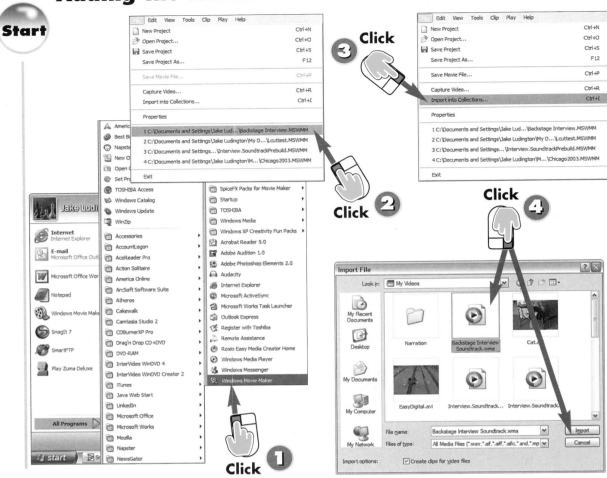

1. Open Movie Maker by clicking **Start**, **All Programs**, **Windows Movie Maker**.

2. Click **File** and select your project from the list of recent projects.

3. Import the normalized audio file by clicking **File**, **Import into Collections**.

4. Choose the normalized audio file you saved in Sound Editor and click **Import**.

Once the audio track has been normalized, it's time to add it to the movie project in Movie Maker. The final audio soundtrack can then be added to the project timeline.

Importing Shortcut
Using the keyboard shortcut **Ctrl+I** launches the Movie Maker import function.

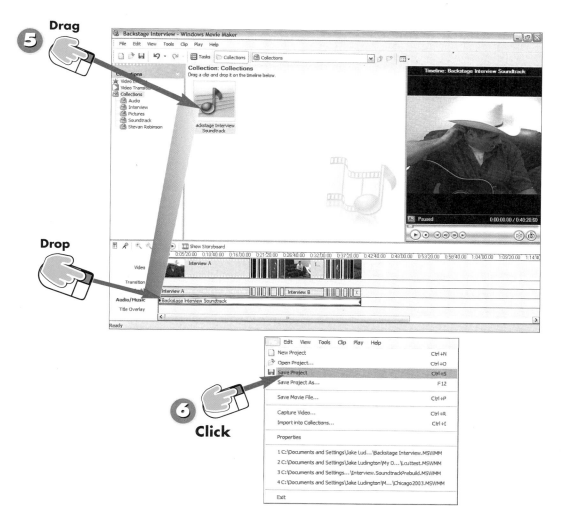

Drag

Drop

Click

⑤ Drag the audio file to the **Audio/Music** section of the timeline, making sure the left edge of the file lines up with the left edge of the movie.

⑥ Save the project file so it includes your audio soundtrack by clicking **File**, **Save Project** on the menu.

End

Editing the Normalized Audio
Normalizing the soundtrack would typically be the last step in editing audio; however, if you need to edit a small section of the audio soundtrack, use the **Split Clip** button under the preview monitor to divide the soundtrack into smaller sections that you can then edit in an outside editor.

Still Photos and Video

Still photos serve a variety of purposes in movie creation. Photos make good backgrounds for title slides. Series of images make great digital slideshows. Pan and zoom effects added to stills create simulated movement. Windows Movie Maker supports the use of stills in all of these ways.

Movie Maker supports most of the common image types, including .GIF, .JPG, and .PNG. These images are added to your Movie Maker project from the hard drive, from a digital camera's memory card, by downloading them from the Internet, or from removable media like CDs and floppies.

Movie Maker includes many effects designed to be used with moving video clips. Pixelan, a third-party developer, complements the Movie Maker effects with a huge selection of effects optimized for use with still images, including a very comprehensive set of pan and zoom effects. These effects are available in the SpiceFX packs from the Pixelan Web site (http://www.pixelan.com/mm/intro.htm).

This part of the book demonstrates various uses for stills in movies, combining Windows Movie Maker and several effects from the Pixelan SpiceFX Pack.

Working With Still Photos

Add Pan/Zoom effects to still images to simulate movement

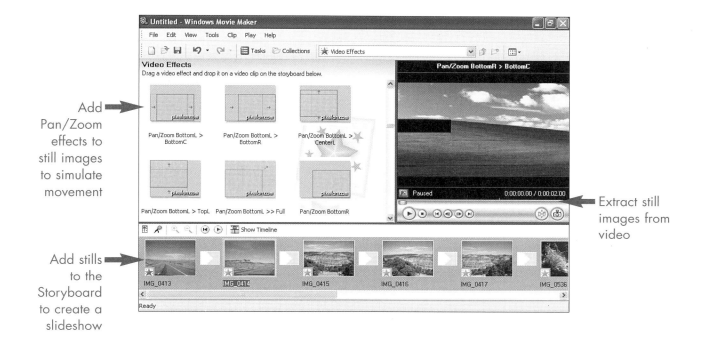

Extract still images from video

Add stills to the Storyboard to create a slideshow

Connecting Your DV Camera via USB

Start

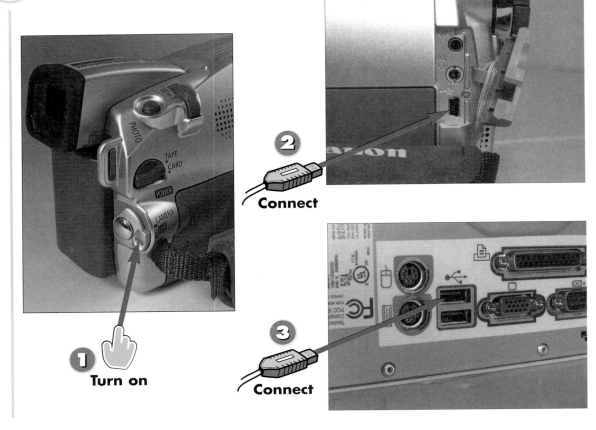

2 Connect

1 Turn on

3 Connect

End

1 Turn the DV Camera on in **Play** mode. (This is usually designated by VCR or VTR.)

2 Locate the USB port on the DV camera and connect the small end of the USB cable.

3 Connect the other end of the USB cable to your PC.

Using a Flash Card Reader

Start

1 Remove card

2 Insert card

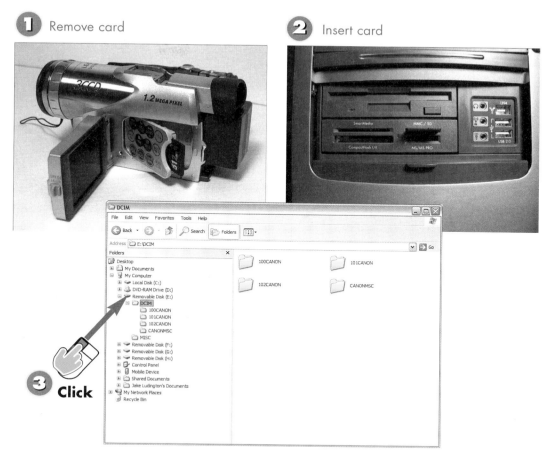

3 Click

1 Remove the memory from your DV camera or digital camera.

2 Insert the memory in the appropriate slot in the reader.

3 Open My Computer or Windows Explorer and click the drive that represents your removable media. Browse folders on the memory card, just as you would any other hard drive.

End

INTRODUCTION
Card readers are an alternative to connecting cables to your camera for extracting images. Card readers come in a variety of styles with support for one or many flash card types.

TIP

External Card Readers
The card reader pictured here comes built-in on many HP computers. A variety of external card readers are available, most of which connect to the computer via USB.

Importing Still Photos

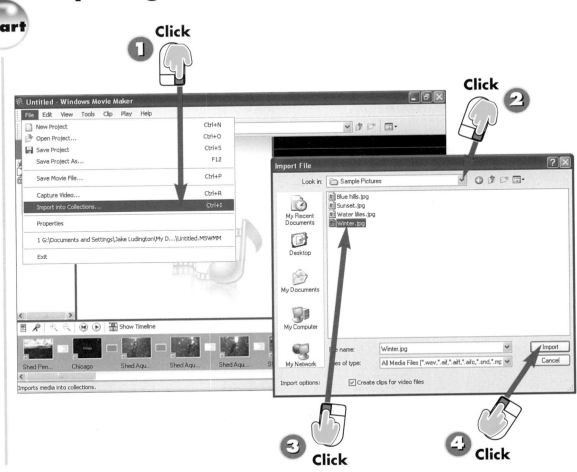

Start

Click ①

Click ②

Click ③

Click ④

① From the **File** menu select **Import into Collections**.

② Click the drop-down list in the Look in field to locate the folder where your picture is located.

③ Select the picture.

④ Click the **Import** button.

End

Creating a Still Photo from Video

Start

Click **1**

Drag **2**

Click **3**

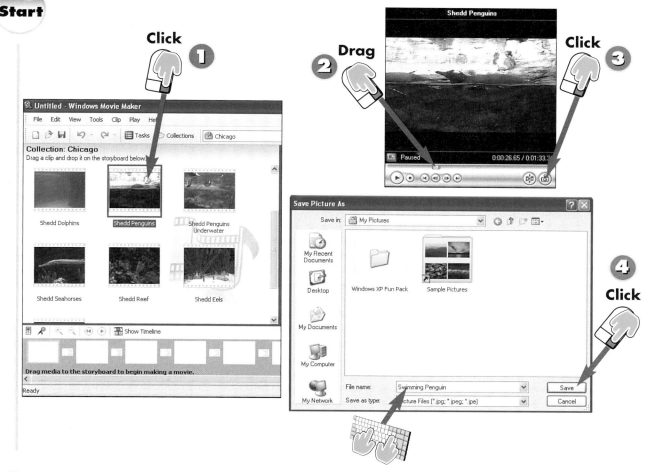

Click **4**

1 In the **Collection** pane, choose the video clip you want to take a picture from.

2 Drag the playback slider under the video monitor until you can see the frame of the video you want to save as a picture.

3 Click the **Take Picture** button.

4 Type a name for the picture and then click the **Save** button.

End

Extracting still photos from video allows you to grab individual movie frames from a video clip. Find the frame in your video clip you want to capture and then extract a picture of it using the Movie Maker monitor pane.

TIP

Optional Method
You can also save still photos from video files on the Timeline by moving the slider to the frame you want to capture and clicking the **Take Picture** button under the preview monitor. The still photos are automatically added to your collection when the image is saved.

Make a Photo Slideshow

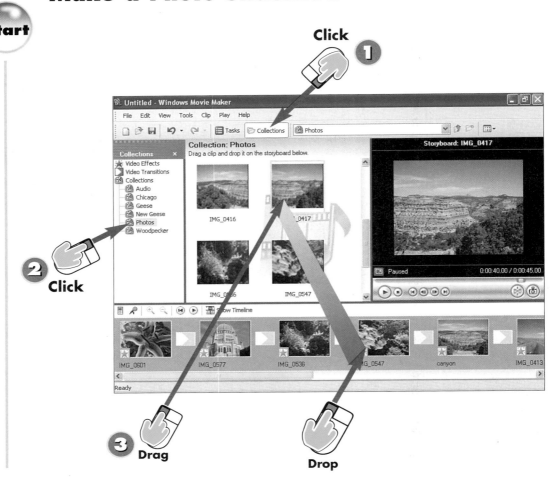

1. Click the **Collections** button on the toolbar.

2. Select the collection containing photos.

3. Drag photos from the collection to the **Storyboard**.

Adding a series of still images to the Windows Movie Maker Storyboard allows you to create a slideshow. This is useful for creating a chronological narrative of a series of events or for making an album of the family vacation.

TIP

Slideshow AutoMovie
Movie Maker's AutoMovie feature will automatically arrange all your pictures for you on the Storyboard. It will also add titles and allow you to choose one audio track for the soundtrack. This is covered in more detail in Part 6, "Editing Video with Windows Movie Maker.

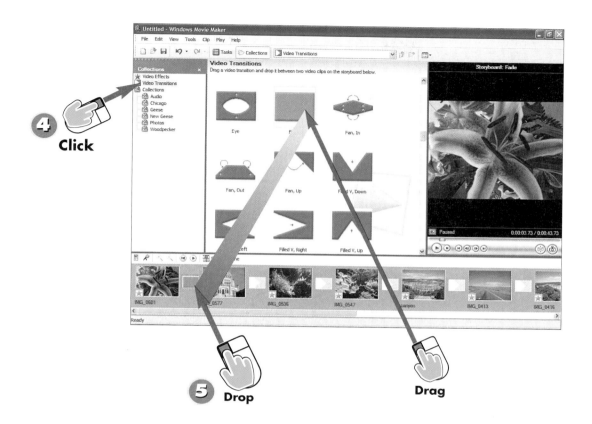

Click

5 **Drop**

Drag

4 Click the **Video Transitions** collection.

5 Drag and drop transitions from the Video Transitions window to the video transition cell between each picture on the Storyboard.

See next page

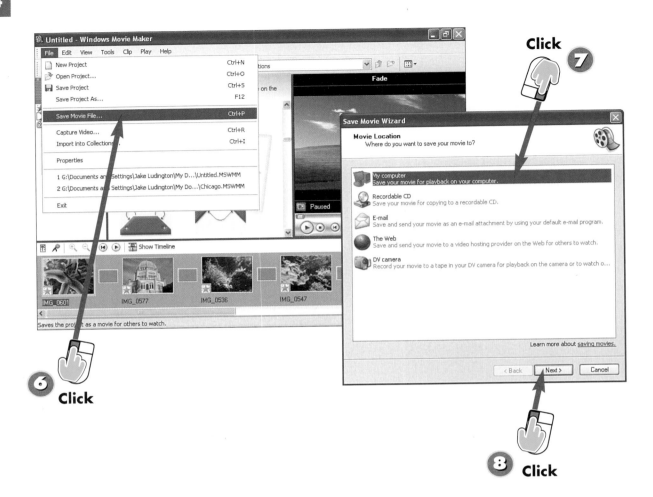

6 Open the **File** menu and click **Save Movie File**.

7 Choose **My Computer**.

8 Click **Next**.

After adding all the transitional elements to your slideshow, it's time to save it as a movie. Depending on who your audience is, you might opt to save multiple versions in different output formats by repeating the save steps.

Narrate Your Slideshow

Transitions aren't the only things you can add to a slideshow. Audio narration and soundtrack audio can also be used to describe each picture. Consult Part 8 on adding audio to your movie for more on these options.

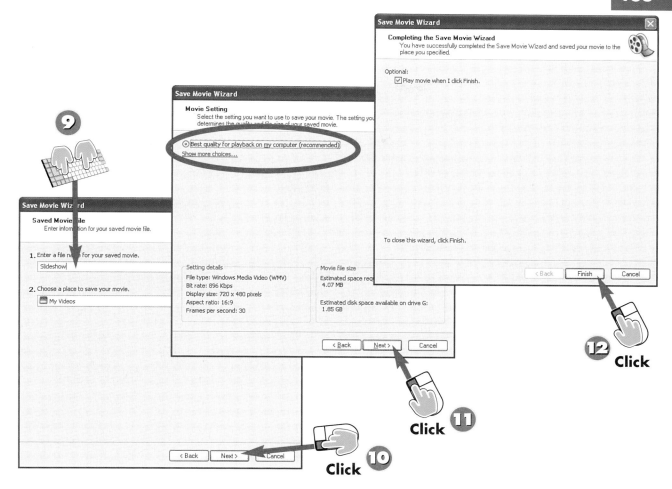

Click

9 Type a name for the slideshow.

10 Click **Next**.

11 Accept the default **Best Quality for playback on my computer (recommended)** and click **Next**.

12 Click **Finish**.

End

Adjusting Picture Display Duration
To extend or reduce the display time for each picture, switch to **Timeline view** and manually stretch the time each picture is onscreen. By default, Movie Maker sets the display time of still images to five seconds.

Changing Default Duration
To change the default duration for displaying pictures, click **Tools**, **Options**. Click the **Advanced** tab, and then adjust the **Picture duration** up or down depending on your needs.

Adding Motion to a Still Image

Start

Click ❶

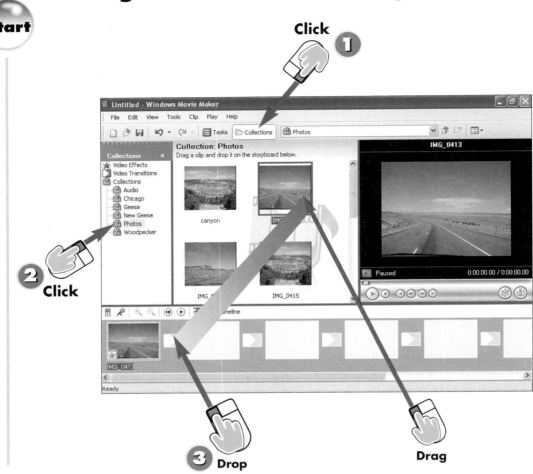

❷ **Click**

❸ **Drop**

Drag

❶ Click the **Collections** button on the toolbar.

❷ Select the collection containing the photo you want to animate from the left **Collections** pane.

❸ Choose the photo and drag it to the **Storyboard**.

TIP

Applying the Same Effect to Multiple Images
To apply the same effect to all images on the Storyboard, first select the effect from the effects collection. Copy the effect using the Ctrl+C keyboard shortcut. Select all pictures on the Storyboard by selecting one and using the Ctrl+A keyboard shortcut, and then Ctrl+P to paste the effect to all images.

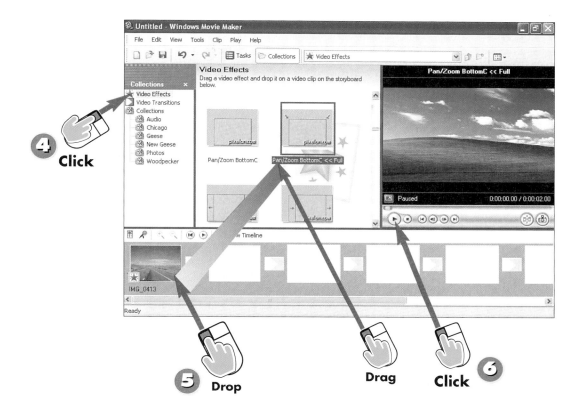

4️⃣ Click the **Video Effects** collection in the left **Collections** pane.

5️⃣ Choose a Pan/Zoom effect from the center **Collections** pane and drag it to the **Storyboard**.

6️⃣ Click the **Play** button on the Monitor to test the Pan/Zoom effect.

End

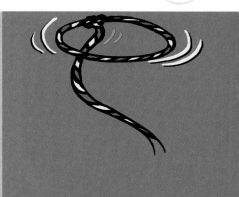

TIP — Multiple effects may be applied to the same photo for a more complex image manipulation. Drag each effect onto the picture to apply additional effects.

TIP — **Video Pan and Zoom** Pan and Zoom effects are most effective when used with still images. While they will technically work with video clips too, the result is generally not desirable.

PART 10

Making DVDs with Sonic MyDVD

So far, the focus has been on creating a movie from video clips and still images. At some point, you will want to share your video with others. Other parts of the book provide steps to share movies electronically. In this part of the book, you learn how to create and burn a DVD.

When you watch a commercially produced DVD from one of the major motion picture studios, you may notice several common elements. Each menu screen includes a *background*, *text links* to the DVD contents, a *menu soundtrack*, and *navigational buttons*. Sonic MyDVD provides tools for creating all these features.

If your PC doesn't have a DVD burner, Sonic MyDVD still provides a solution for distributing your finished movie in a professional-looking package by allowing you to save it as a VCD using a CD burner. VCDs are very similar to DVDs, in that they support an organized menu structure; however, due to the space limitations of burnable CDs (650–700MB compared with the standard 4.7GB found on a DVD), the image quality of a VCD is more comparable to VHS video.

After adding your finished movie to a DVD project, MyDVD provides tools to create navigational menus, customize buttons for accessing special features, insert special features, and burn the completed DVD or VCD. By the time you finish this section, you will have created a complete DVD menu structure and burned a DVD or VCD.

Sonic MyDVD for DVD Authoring

Change background styles

Add movies to your DVD

Create Submenus for extra features

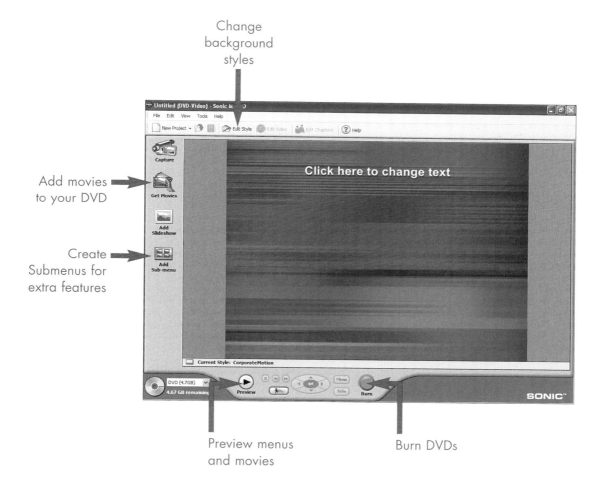

Preview menus and movies

Burn DVDs

Starting Sonic MyDVD

Start

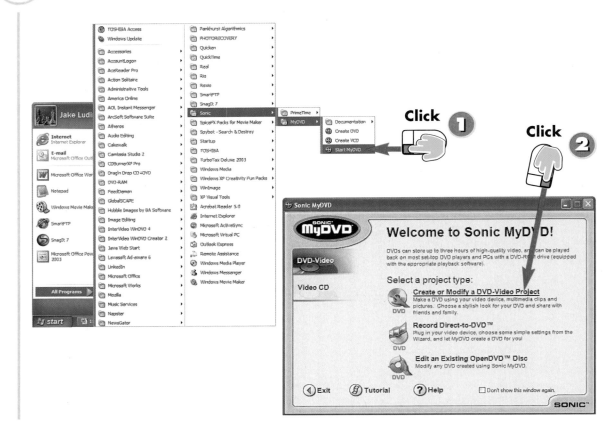

Click ①

Click ②

① Open MyDVD by clicking **Start**, **All Programs**, and then locate the **Sonic** folder and choose **MyDVD**, **Start MyDVD**.

② Click **Create or Modify a DVD-Video Project**.

End

Don't Show This

TIP

Clicking **Don't show this window again** on the MyDVD welcome screen will result in the program opening to a new project each time it is launched, instead of offering you choices. To restore this welcome screen, choose **Preferences** from the **File** menu, and check the box next to **Show the wizard everytime MyDVD starts** in the **Wizard** section of the General preferences tab.

Inserting Movies in a DVD Project

Start

Click ②

Click ①

Click ③

1. Click **Get Movies**.

2. Browse to the folder where your movie file is stored.

3. Select the movie file and click **Open**.

End

TIP

Add Multiple Movies
MyDVD allows you to add as many movies as a DVD will hold. To see how much space is available on the DVD, look at the bottom left corner of the MyDVD project space, which indicates how much space is remaining on the disk.

INFO

Changing the Main Menu Text

Start

Click **1**

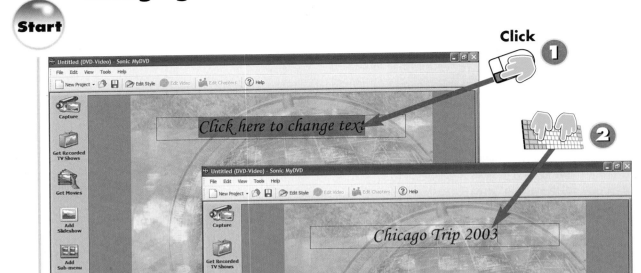

2

1 Click the text on the menu screen to add your own text.

2 Type in the text space to create your own menu title.

End

TIP

Opening a Saved Project
By default, MyDVD saves project files in a folder called MyDVDs under your My Documents folder. You can open a saved project by browsing to this folder from the Open File dialog box (**File**, **Open**) and clicking **Open**. Or you can open a project by double-clicking on its .dvd project file in the MyDVDs folder.

Changing the Main Menu Style

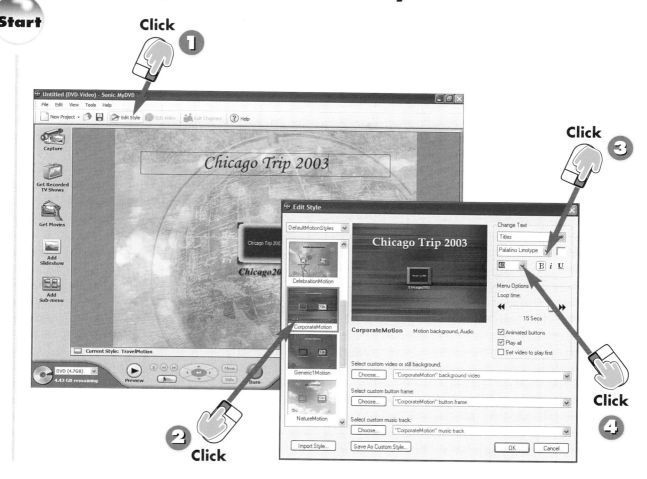

Start

Click 1

Click 2

Click 3

Click 4

1. Click the **Edit Style** button on the toolbar.

2. Select a style from the list on the left side of the window.

3. Change the Menu title font by selecting from the Font drop-down list under **Change Text**.

4. Adjust the Menu title font size by choosing a new size under **Change Text**.

End

INTRODUCTION

DVD menus simplify the navigation of the movie content and extras on a DVD. MyDVD menu styles allow you to customize the appearance of your DVD menus. Each element of the style may be changed either in a style group or individually.

TIP

Create a Custom Menu Style
To reuse your style settings in future projects, click the **Save As Custom Style** when all your changes are complete.

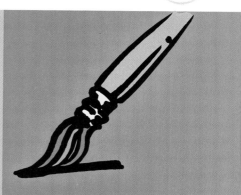

Customizing Menu Buttons

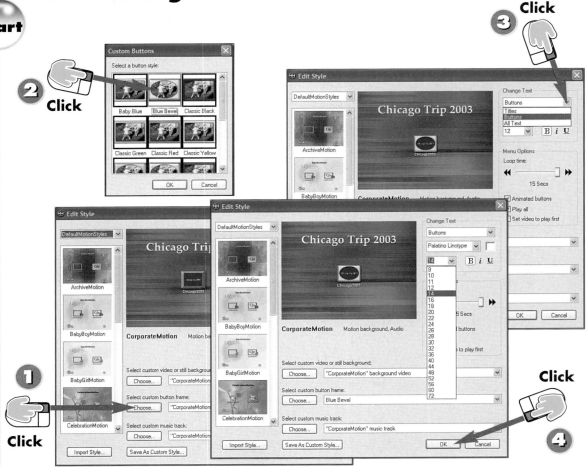

Start

Click 2

Click 3

Click 4

Click 1

Click

1. Under Select custom button frame, click the **Choose** button.

2. Select a new button frame style from the list of choices and click **OK**.

3. Modify the button font by selecting **Buttons** from the top **Change Text** drop-down menu.

4. Select a new font and size from the drop-down menus under **Change Text**. Click **OK**.

End

Adding a Custom Menu Soundtrack

Start

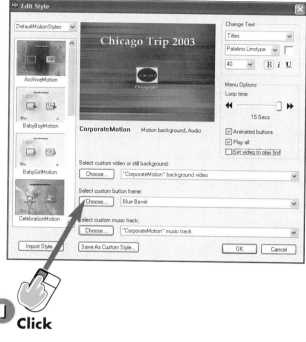

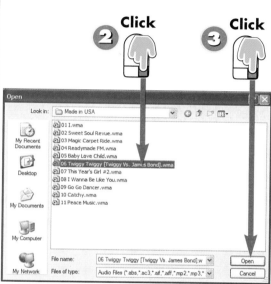

Click ②

Click ③

Click ①

1. Click the **Edit Style** button to open the Edit Style dialog box and then click the **Choose** button under Select custom music track.

2. Browse to the folder where the audio clip is located.

3. Select the audio clip and click **Open**.

End

INTRODUCTION

DVD menus often include audio either excerpted from the full soundtrack or specifically tailored to the menu. Customize the audio on your menus to achieve a more robust experience for viewers. Audio is not a required element of the menu screens and can be eliminated if preferred.

HINT

Menu Audio Duration
Menu loop time is limited to 15 seconds. Choosing a short selection or clipping an instrumental segment of a song will sound better than importing a full song.

HINT

Movie Maker Audio
For a customized menu audio track, save out the audio from your movie maker project as a .WMA file and then add it to your custom menu in MyDVD.

Creating Chapters in a Movie

Start

Click ②

Click ①

① Click the movie button in the center of the project space to select it.

② Click the **Edit Chapters** button on the toolbar.

INTRODUCTION

Chapters allow movie viewers to skip to favorite parts of the movie or quickly pick up where they left off. Chapter markers are reference points used by a DVD player's operating system to jump to a specific point in a movie. MyDVD allows you to create chapters in your movie so finding a specific scene is easier.

TIP

Play All
The Edit Styles menu includes a **Play All** check box. If this is checked, MyDVD configures the DVD to play all content on the DVD before returning to the main menu. Unchecking this box causes the DVD to return to the menu screen after each feature executes, similar to the behavior of special features on consumer DVD titles.

Click 4

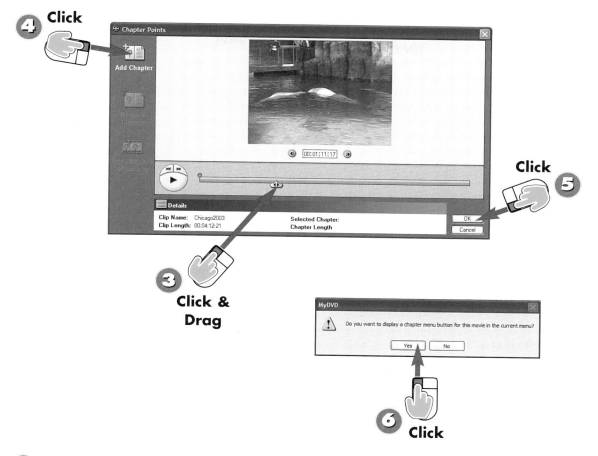

Click 5

3
**Click &
Drag**

6 **Click**

3 Click and drag the slider to the desired chapter point.

4 Click the **Add Chapter** button. Repeat steps 3 and 4 until all chapter points are added.

5 Click **OK**.

6 Click **Yes** to create a chapter menu button in your menu.

End

Chapters 101

Clicking the play button on the DVD plays the entire movie in full. Starting the movie from a chapter point begins playback at the beginning of that chapter and continues through the end of the movie.

Where Did the Movie Button Go?

Creating a chapter menu button will hide the Movie button. To restore the Movie button, right-click the chapter button and select **Copy** from the menu. Right-click again and choose **Paste**. Click on the button copy and select **View as Movie Button** from the **View** menu.

Editing Chapter Titles

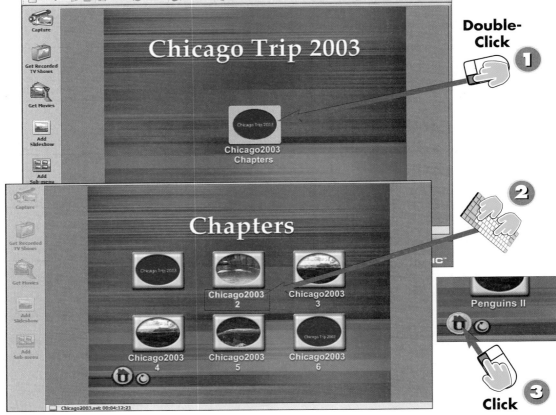

Double-Click 1

2

Click 3

Start

End

1. Double-click the movie chapter button on the main menu screen.

2. Click the title under a chapter button and type a new name for the chapter.

3. Return to the main menu level by double-clicking the **Home** button.

INTRODUCTION

Sonic MyDVD labels each chapter using the movie title plus an incremental number. To give the chapters more meaningful names, edit them on the chapter submenu.

TIP

Chapters Menu
MyDVD automatically adds the word Chapters to the title of the Chapters screen. For instance, if you simply wanted the title to say *Chapters* and typed the word Chapters, MyDVD would add *Chapters* to the end of the title, making it *Chapters Chapters*. To get around this, leaving the title blank results in MyDVD defaulting to the word *Chapters* as the title for the screen.

Adding Submenus

Start

Click ❶

1. Click the **Add Sub-menu** button.

2. Click the text under your new button and type a descriptive name for the menu.

End

INTRODUCTION

DVD menus frequently contain submenus where extras such as picture slideshows, deleted scenes, and chapter selections are stored. Adding additional menu layers organizes your DVD menu system even further.

Adding a Slideshow

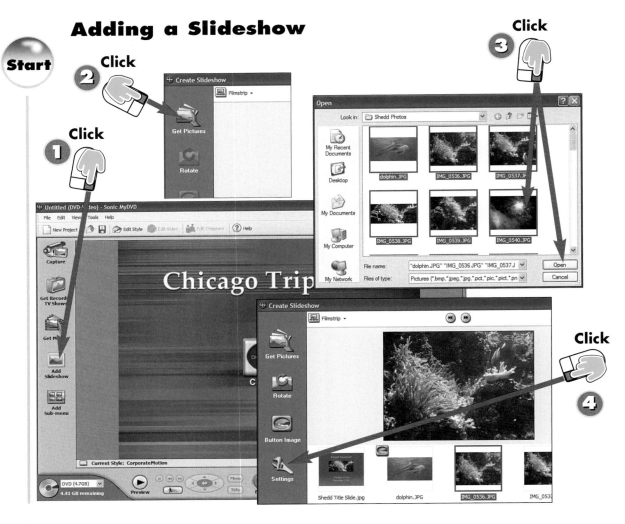

Start

Click ①

Click ②

Click ③

Click ④

---

① Click the **Add Slideshow** button.

② Click the **Get Pictures** button to browse for photos.

③ Navigate to the folder containing pictures you want to include in the slideshow. Select the pictures you want to include and then click **Open**.

④ Click the **Settings** button to customize the slideshow.

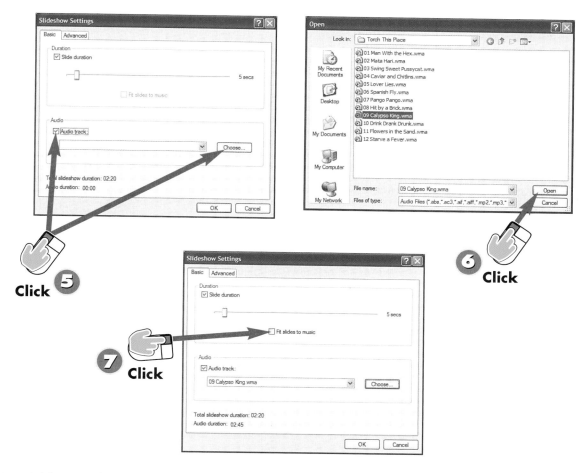

5. Add an audio track to the slide show by checking the box next to **Audio track** and then clicking the **Choose** button next to the audio selection drop-down.

6. Select a music track and click **Open**.

7. Check the box next to **Fit slides to music** to synchronize the slides to the music.

See next page

TIP

Removing Unwanted Images
To remove an unwanted image from a slideshow, scroll through the list of images in the slideshow, highlight the image, and press the **Delete** key on the keyboard.

HINT

Organizing Images
To change the order of images in the slideshow, click and drag an image from its current location to the location you want it to appear in the slideshow. By default, MyDVD organizes photos alphabetically by filename.

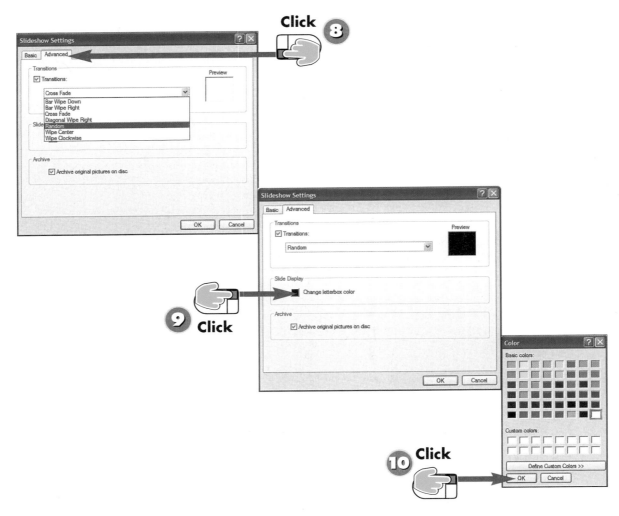

Click 8

9 **Click**

Click 10

---

8 Click the **Advanced** tab to change the transition between images, and select a transition from the drop-down menu.

9 Click **Change letterbox color**.

10 Select a letterbox background color. This determines the background color for images smaller than full screen. Click **OK**.

Slideshow creation in MyDVD allows you to customize virtually every aspect of the slideshow. After picking music and selecting transition styles for the slideshow, the slideshow is added to the DVD project.

TIP

No Transition Between Photos
MyDVD does not require the use of transitions between slides. To turn off transitions, click the **Advanced** tab of the Settings window and uncheck the box next to **Transitions**.

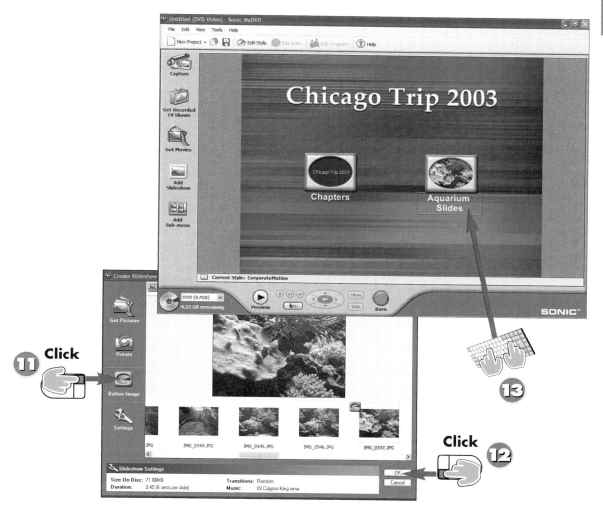

(11) Highlight an image in the slideshow and click the **Button Image** button to set the image to be displayed on the slideshow menu button.

(12) Click **OK** to add the slideshow to the DVD project.

(13) Click the text under the slideshow button and type a new title for the slideshow.

End

Additional Slideshows
MyDVD projects can contain more than one slideshow. After completing one slideshow, repeat the steps of this task to add additional slideshows to the DVD project.

Photo Archive
MyDVD includes an option to archive the original photos on disk. This uses more space than only including the slideshow, but also creates a handy backup of the image files in case the versions on your hard drive get damaged.

Burning a DVD

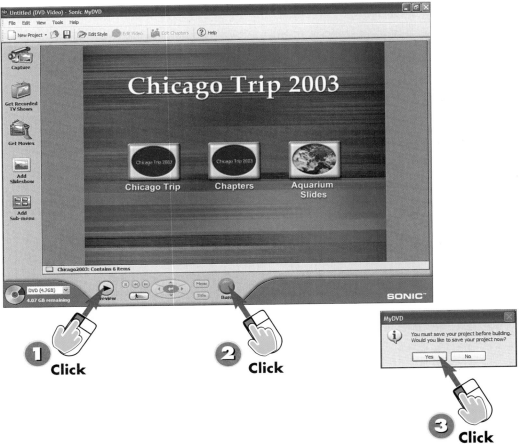

Start

1 Click

2 Click

3 Click

1 Click the **Preview** button and test the various menu buttons.

2 When you are satisfied everything works, click the red **Burn** button.

3 Click **Yes** to save the DVD project.

INTRODUCTION

Once all the menus are created, it's finally time to make the DVD. MyDVD processes all the menu customizations, movie data, and slideshow details, outputting a standard DVD designed to play in most consumer DVD players.

Preview Menu

TIP

The MyDVD preview is fully functional, except for the animated menu screen. To preview the menu animation and to see the video preview on the button you have to click the **build motion** menu button (the running man) on the preview interface.

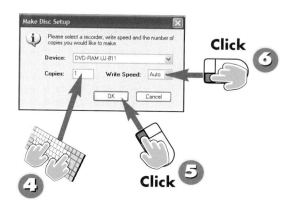

Click 6

4

Click 5

4 Select the number of **Copies** to create.

5 Choose a DVD **Write Speed** from the drop-down list.

6 Click **OK**.

End

Which Write Speed?
Make sure the write speed selected is supported by the blank DVD in the drive. MyDVD automatically detects the fastest speed of the DVD burner. Choosing a speed faster than the blank disk supports could result in a "coaster" instead of a usable DVD.

Slow Burn
In general, burning DVDs at the slowest supported setting is recommended. Each disk will take longer to burn, but the likelihood of having corrupt data on the disk is reduced.

Burning a VCD

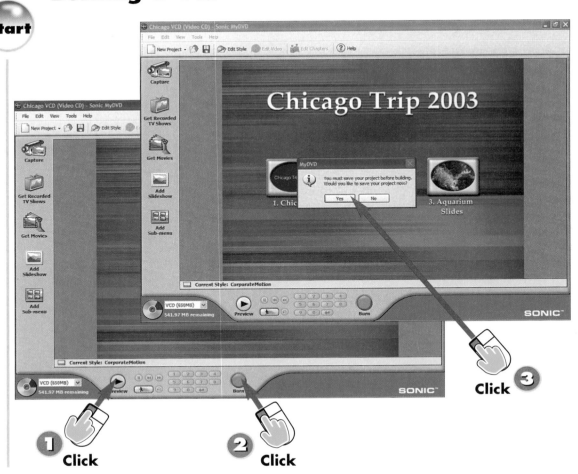

Start

Click 1

Click 2

Click 3

1) Click the **Preview** button and test the various menu buttons.

2) When you are satisfied everything works, click the red **Burn** button.

3) Click **Yes** to save the VCD project.

The process of creating a VCD using MyDVD is identical to the process of creating a DVD. The quality of output is very different. Burning a DVD results in image quality on par with what the video looks like on your hard drive. VCDs are limited to VHS quality images and can only store 650–700MB of data instead of a DVD's 4.7GB.

VCD Slideshows

The slideshow feature of MyDVD works in both DVD and VCD project modes. However, the VCD format does not support the addition of transitions or audio to slideshows, so VCD slideshows lack some of the flash found in their DVD counterparts.

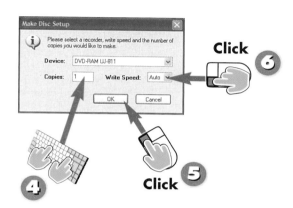

4 Select the number of **Copies** to create.

5 Choose a DVD **Write Speed** from the drop-down list.

6 Click **OK**.

VCDs and Older DVD Players
While most DVD players manufactured in the last 2–3 years support VCDs burned to CD-R media, this hasn't always been the case. Older DVD players often do not support VCD and in some cases won't support burned DVDs either.

Universal Playback
If the target audience for your movie is made up of PC owners, burning movies in the HighMAT CD format described earlier in the book is a much more universal option. It may not play back on all home DVD players, but it should play on virtually every Windows desktop. VCDs won't play in many PC software DVD applications, which means if the VCD doesn't work in your neighbor's DVD player, it might not work in their PC either, leaving the neighbor unable to watch your movie at all.

Sharing Movies with Streaming Video

Streaming video is available on many sites across the Internet. If you've ever watched a news clip on CNN.com or watched sports highlights at ESPN.com, you've seen streaming video in action. If you have Web space provided by your ISP, or if you have a Web site, sharing home movies on the Web makes sense.

Video files are often too large to send through email, although Movie Maker provides settings which optimize video for email very effectively. You'll learn how to use these settings in this part of the book. Video takes up space on email servers, causing the people who administer email accounts to limit allowed file sizes for incoming files or block attachments altogether due to concerns about viruses.

Posting video to a Web site is a great way to avoid the headaches of sending video through email. Instead of mailing friends and family a big file, you send a link to the page where the video resides and they can either watch the video online or download it to their hard drives.

After constructing a movie with sound, transitions, edited video clips, and effects, saving the movie in a format usable by the intended audience is the next logical step. Windows Movie Maker includes many preconfigured options designed to make saving movies painless. Streaming video, email, and Pocket PC playback are some of the more common options.

This part of the book shows you how to save and distribute your movie via the Web, email, and Pocket PC.

Options for Saving Movies in Movie Maker

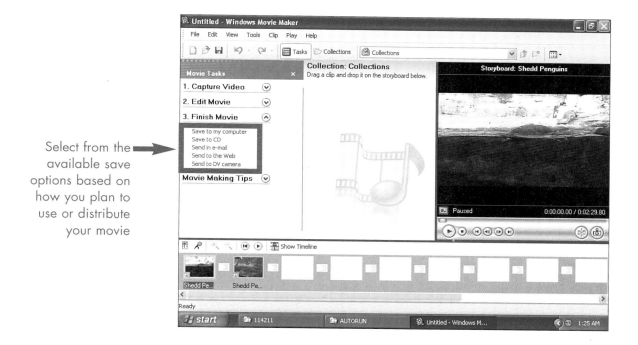

Select from the available save options based on how you plan to use or distribute your movie

Saving a Movie for Sharing Via Email

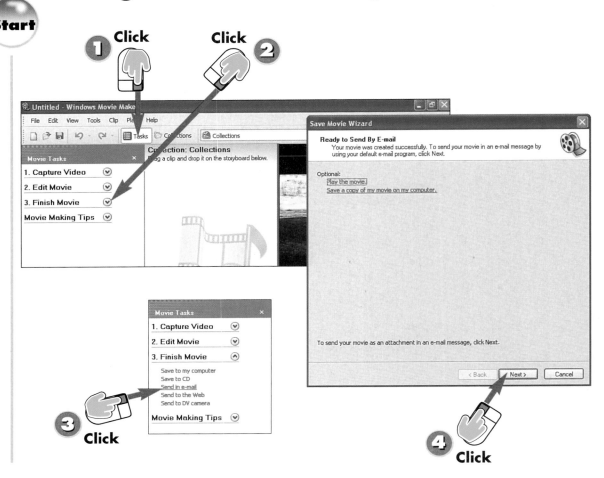

Start

Click ①

Click ②

③ Click

④ Click

---

① With the movie you want to send via email open, click **Tasks** on the toolbar.

② Expand the **Finish Movie** section by clicking the down arrow.

③ Click **Send in e-mail**.

④ Wait while Movie Maker saves the movie. Click **Next** to send the movie using your default email client.

Email is one obvious way to share your movie with friends and relatives. Windows Movie Maker simplifies the process of emailing movies through some predefined settings. Unlike still images, movie files can be hundreds of megabytes, or sometimes gigabytes in size. This makes sending uncompressed video via email almost impossible.

HINT

Email Video Quality
Don't expect the email-ready version of your movie to look as good as the uncompressed version used to make DVDs. In order to shrink the file size, Movie Maker must reduce the quality of certain elements within the movie.

Click

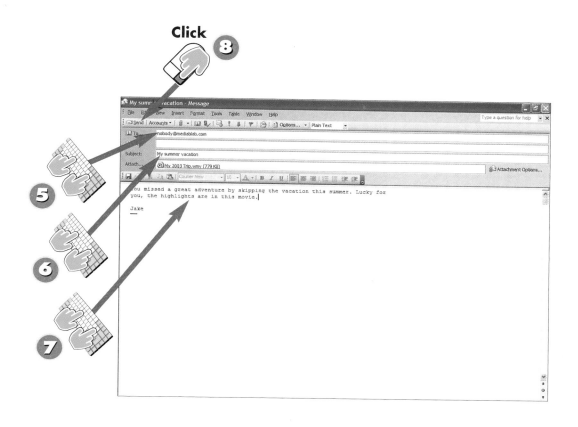

5 Type the email address of the person who will receive your movie in the **To** field.

6 Change the message **Subject** to match the subject of your message.

7 Type a message to the recipient.

8 Click **Send**.

End

Limit Movie Length
Unless all your recipients have high-speed Internet access, it is recommended you limit the length of emailed movies to fewer than five minutes. It's a good idea to send a message before the attachment warning the user that a large file is on its way.

Avoid Special Effects
When you know a video will be sent via email, avoid using lots of fancy effects and transitions. While they look cool, they also greatly increase the size of the final video.

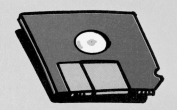

Saving a Movie for the Web

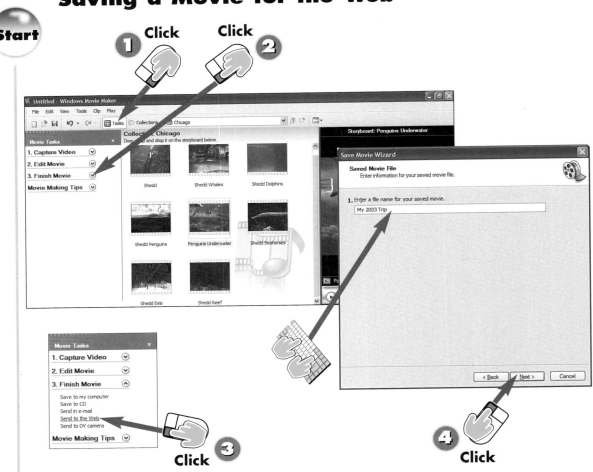

Start

Click ❶

Click ❷

Click ❸

Click ❹

❶ With the movie to be saved for the Web open, click **Tasks** on the toolbar.

❷ Expand the **Finish Movie** section by clicking the down arrow.

❸ Click **Send to the Web**.

❹ Type a name for your movie and click **Next**.

PART 11

Storing large movie files on the Web for downloading will keep friends and family from getting a "mailbox full" message. Most ISPs provide some amount of free space, which is great for hosting streaming video for small audiences, but may not be enough for larger projects. Movie Maker's Save for the Web option ties into the Neptune Mediashare hosting service (http://www.neptune.com) designed to support larger video file sizes for registered users.

Skip the Cost

If you prefer not to pay the yearly subscription fee for Mediashare, you can simply save the movie files to your hard drive rather than using the Save for Web option, and then you can upload the files anywhere.

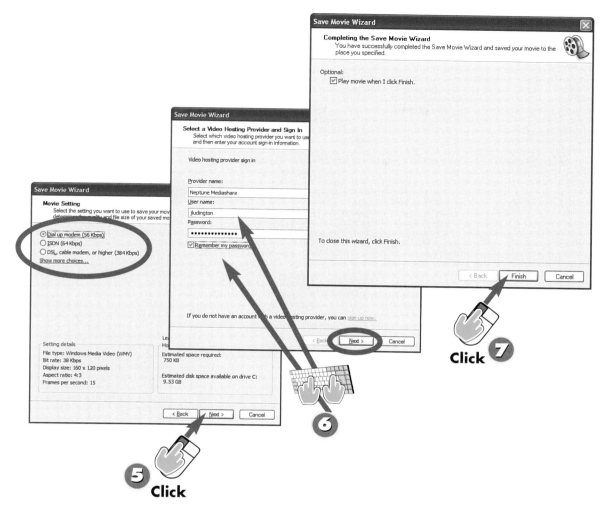

Click 7

5 Click

6

5 Select a video playback quality from the list and click **Next**.

6 Type in your Neptune Mediashare username and password and click Next.

7 Check the box to view your video online and click **Finish**.

End

Which Video Quality?

If most of the people watching your movie are AOL users or use a dial-up account, choose **Dial up modem**, or expect to get complaints about the video not playing. If you are certain most of the people receiving your video have cable or DSL connections, select one of the faster speeds for better video quality. Depending on which quality setting you selected and the speed of your Internet connection, uploading the file to Neptune Mediashare may take a few seconds, several minutes, or even an hour. In general, it's better to attempt this only if you have a high-speed Internet connection.

Uploading a Movie to the Web Using SmartFTP

Start

Click **1**

Click **2**

Click **3**

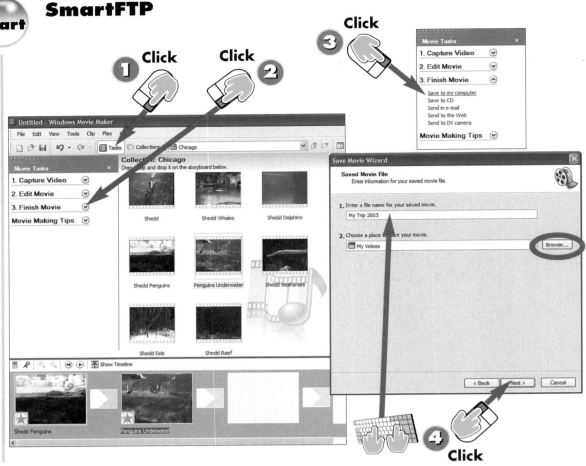

Click **4**

1 With the movie to be saved for the Web open, click **Tasks** on the toolbar.

2 Expand the **Finish Movie** section by clicking the down arrow.

3 Click **Save to my computer**.

4 Type a name for your movie and, optionally, choose a different location to save the file to. Click **Next**.

Before we can upload a movie with a file transfer program, the movie needs to be saved to the hard drive. Movie Maker defaults to the My Videos folder when saving, which is easy to remember when browsing for the file later during the transfer. Choosing a video quality setting similar to the one used for Saving to the Web in the previous task is ideal for this type of upload because the file is still being hosted on a Web server, just not on the Movie Maker recommended site.

TIP

Consider Your Users
Before choosing a movie quality setting, consider who will be watching. If the audience is mostly dial-up users with AOL or Earthlink accounts, choose a dial-up option. If the audience consists of cable Internet users, a broadband setting will be acceptable.

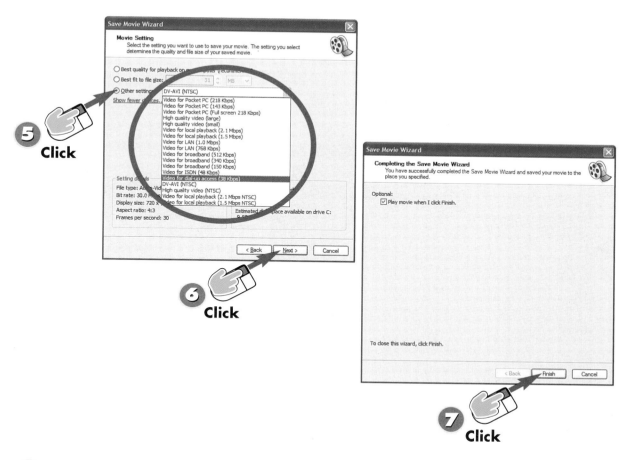

Click 5

Click 6

Click 7

5 Click **Other Settings**.

6 Choose video quality from the drop-down list based on the type of connection viewers will need, and then click **Next**.

7 Click **Finish**.

See next page

Save Multiple Versions
You might have visitors with different access capabilities. You can accommodate both by saving the movie in two different formats, one for dial-up and one for broadband. This gives users with faster connections a better quality movie.

Respect Copyrights
Because the Web is a very public medium, it's important to be extremely careful when posting audio and video files for download. If someone else owns the copyright or distribution rights to a piece of music or video clip used in your movie, don't post the movie on the Web. If you aren't sure whether someone owns the rights, assume someone does and avoid posting the file to the Web.

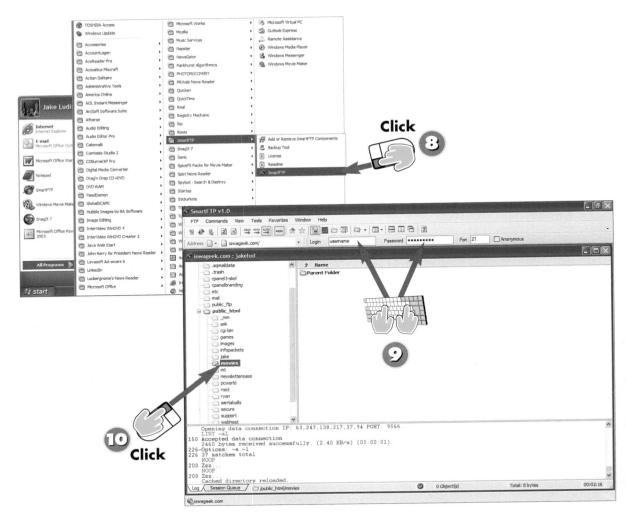

8 Open SmartFTP by clicking **Start**, **All Programs**, **SmartFTP**, **SmartFTP**.

9 Type your server name, username, and password in the appropriate Address toolbar fields and press **Enter**.

10 In the pane on the left, select the folder on the server where the movie will be uploaded.

To make a movie available for download, it needs to be transferred from your computer to the server where it will be hosted. Uploading files is commonly done with an FTP client. SmartFTP is a shareware FTP application, free to home users, available from www.smartftp.com.

Who Watches Your Movie
The Web is a public place, so you have no idea who might find your movie. Be careful what you upload to the Web. If you would be embarrassed or offended if co-workers or complete strangers found your movie, it's probably best not to host it on the Web.

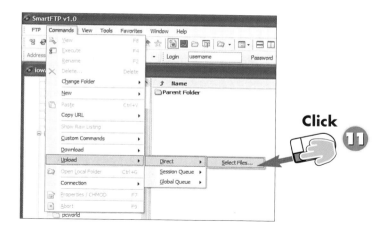

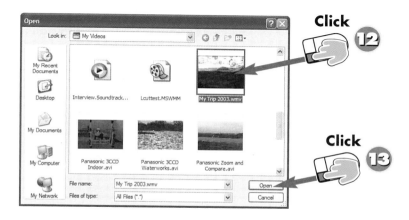

Click 11

Click 12

Click 13

11 From the **View** menu choose **Upload**, **Direct**, **Select Files.**

12 Browse to the location of the movie on your hard drive and click the movie to select it.

13 Click **Open**.

End

Remember Where the File Is
Earlier in this task, we saved the movie file to the My Videos folder in My Documents. If you can't find your movie file, try looking in that folder.

Test the Link
Before emailing the link where the video file you uploaded is located, test it out. Better to find out you made a mistake entering the URL or that the video file isn't displaying properly before you announce its location.

Saving Movies for Pocket PC Playback

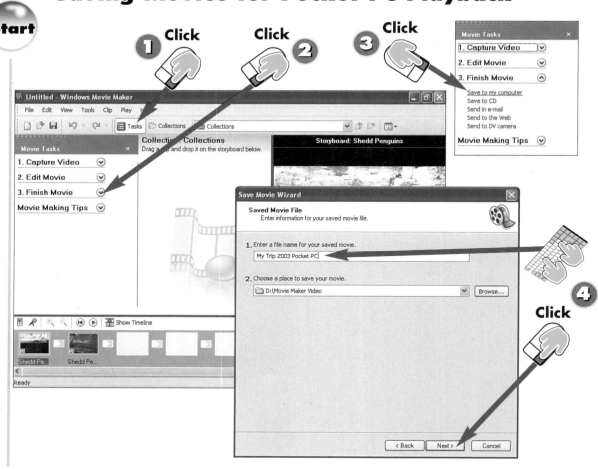

Start

Click 1 **Click 2** **Click 3**

Click 4

1. Click **Tasks** on the toolbar.

2. Expand the **Finish Movie** section by clicking the down arrow.

3. Click **Save to my computer**.

4. Type a name for your movie and click **Next**.

INTRODUCTION

Many people now own Pocket PC devices, which support video playback. Windows Movie Maker includes custom save settings optimized for playing on Pocket PC devices, which shrinks the image dimensions to fit a Pocket PC screen as well as reduce the overall file size.

TIP

Pocket PC options
Unless your Pocket PC memory card is short on space, it's best to use the full screen save setting. This results in the best quality image for Pocket PC screens and it also makes viewing the movie much more enjoyable because no squinting is required.

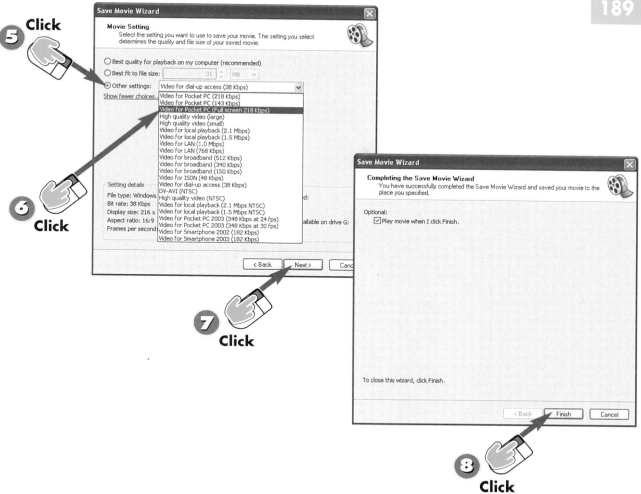

5 Click **Other Settings**.

6 Choose **Video for Pocket PC (Full screen 218 Kbps)** from the drop-down list.

7 Click **Next**.

8 Click **Finish**.

End

HINT
If your Pocket PC has limited space on its removable media, choose one of the other preconfigured Pocket PC save options to conserve space.

TIP
Don't Play
Uncheck the **Play movie when I click Finish** check box if you don't want to preview the Pocket PC version of your movie.

Transferring Movies to a Pocket PC

Start

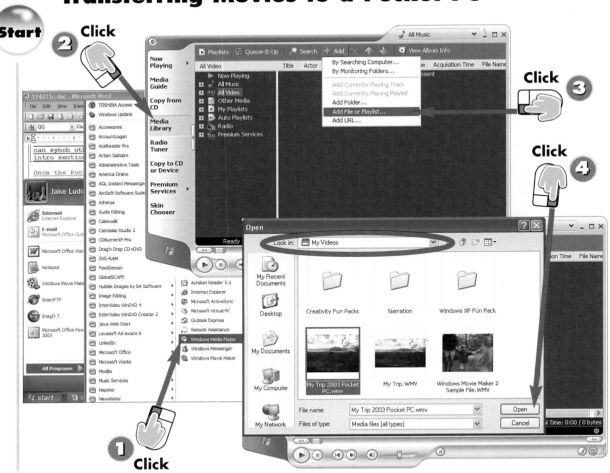

Click 2

Click 3

Click 4

Click 1

① With the Pocket PC on its cradle, click **Start**, **All Programs**, **Windows Media Player**.

② Click **Media Library**.

③ Click the **Add** button, and then choose **Add File or Playlist**.

④ Click the arrow in the Look in field to browse to the location of your video and select it, then click **Open**.

INTRODUCTION

Once the Pocket PC movie is completed, it's time to transfer it to your portable device. The easiest way to transfer movies from your desktop to a Pocket PC is via Windows Media Player. Movies can also be added using the standard activesync software and either a wireless connection or the device's docking station.

TIP

Other Media Files

If your Pocket PC supports audio playback, Windows Media Player also works for transferring songs and books on tape to Pocket PC devices. This is particularly useful on models with Compact Flash or SD slots, providing all the features of a portable media player without needing yet another device.

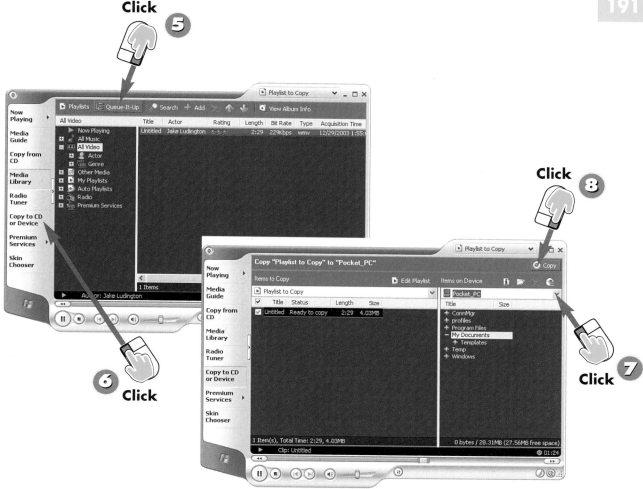

Click 5

Click 8

Click 7

Click 6

5 Click **Queue-It-Up**.

6 Click **Copy to a CD or Device**.

7 Select the Pocket PC or its Storage Card from the **Items on Device** menu.

8 Check the box next to the movie under **Playlist to Copy**, and then click **Copy**.

End

If you have several videos to transfer all at once, create a Windows Movie Maker Playlist and transfer the entire playlist.

Not All PDAs Are Equal
Unfortunately, Palm OS devices don't currently support WMV playback. If your PDA uses Palm OS, you'll either need to switch to the dark side, or find another format for making portable home movies.

Glossary

A

Audio Level   An alternative term for audio volume.

AVI   Abbreviation for Audio Video Interleaved, this is the standard Windows format for delivering uncompressed video.

B

Bit   Short for binary digit, this is the smallest unit of data recognized by a PC.

Bit Rate   The number of bits transferred per second.

C

Capture   Recording audio, video, or still images as digital information in a movie project file.

Capture Device   Hardware used in transferring audio and video from an external source, such as a camcorder or VCR, to a computer.

Clip   A segment of a video extracted from a larger video file.

Codec   Software or hardware used to compress and decompress digital media.

Collection   A file container within Windows Movie Maker used to organize video clips, images, and audio.

Compression

Compression   The process of reducing a file size by removing redundant information from the file.

Cross-fade   A video transition method where the frames in the current clip fade out as frames in the new clip fade in.

D

Digital8   Sony's proprietary digital video format, which is backward compatible with Hi8. This format uses standard 8mm tape to record and store video data.

Digital Artifacts   Distorted areas in a video or image file, often appearing as square shapes within the picture.

Digital Camcorder   A device for recording video in a digital format. Common digital camcorders capture video in mini-DV, Digital8, and DVD MPEG-2 formats.

Digital Video (DV)   Video and sound stored in a digital format.

DV-AVI   An uncompressed Microsoft audio/video format used to encode camcorder data into a format usable by Windows Movie Maker.

E-F

Effect   A special effect applied to video footage in Windows Movie Maker.

Fade   A transitional effect designed to bring the video from or to black by gradually decreasing or increasing light in the picture.

FireWire (See also i.Link and IEEE 1394)   A high-speed data serial transfer standard providing connectivity for a wide range of devices, including camcorders, external hard drives, and portable media devices.

Frame   One single image in the series of images making up a video.

Frame Rate   The number of video frames displayed per second. Most DV camcorders record video at 29.97 frames per second. In general, the higher the frame rate the smoother the picture.

G-I

IEEE 1394 (See also FireWire and iLink)   A high-speed data serial transfer standard providing connectivity for a wide range of devices, including camcorders, external hard drives, and portable media devices.

i.LINK (See also FireWire and IEEE 1394)   The Sony implementation of IEEE 1394.

K-M

Line Noise   Unwanted noise in an audio track caused by electrical currents interfering with the transmission of audio data through a cable.

Microphone Noise   Unwanted sound captured when a microphone is bumped during recording.

Mini-DV   The format common to most digital video camcorders, which uses 6.35mm tape to record and store video data.

N-R

NTSC   National Television Standards Committee. This is most commonly referenced in terms of the technical standard for video formatting in the United States.

PAL   Phase Alternative Line. A competing standards body to NTSC. Most of the world outside the U.S. conforms to video standards based on PAL.

Project File   The master file used by Windows Movie Maker to store information about imported data and how it is arranged within the project.

S

Source   Device containing audio and video content to be captured and encoded by Windows Movie Maker.

Split   Dividing one larger audio or video clip into two smaller clips.

Storyboard   A layout of a Windows Movie Maker project displaying video clips, transitions, and effects sequentially in a simplified workspace.

Super 8   A film format introduced by Kodak in 1965, which uses 8mm cartridge-loaded film reels for recording movies.

S-Video   Sometimes referred to as S-VHS, this video transmission format separates black-and-white video information from color data into two signals. Traditional composite video sends this information as one signal.

T-V

Timeline   A detailed workspace view of a Windows Movie Maker project showing relative lengths of each element used within the project and how they overlap.

Transition   A transition is a special kind of effect placed between two movie clips to enhance the progression of the movie's story as it moves to the next scene.

Trim   Hiding parts of an audio or video clip in the project space without permanently removing them from the source file. Audio and video clips can be trimmed by adjusting the start or end trim points, which alters playback within the project, while leaving the original file intact.

Trim Points   Markers on the timeline of a project file designating the starting and ending points for a particular media clip.

W-Z

Windows Media file   A file containing audio, video, or script data stored in Windows Media Format. Depending on content and purpose, Windows Media files use a variety of filename extensions, including: .wma, .wme, .wms, .wmv, .wmx, .wmz, or .wvx. Most Windows Movie Maker projects deal with .wma and .wmv files.

Workspace   The area of Windows Movie Maker where movies are pieced together. The workspace is made up of two views: storyboard and timeline.

Zoom   Magnifying or shrinking the image viewed by a camera lens, making the object appear closer or farther than it actually is in physical space.

Index

Numbers

16:9 format, 26

4:3 format, 27

8mm projection movies

recording sound, 35

recording with DV cameras, 35

A

accessory shoe, 5

adding

audio tracks to slideshows, 171

credits, 102-103

custom menu soundtracks to DVD projects, 165

dissolves, 92-93

effects to movie clips, 115

fades, 94-95

motion to still images, 156-157

movie clips to video, 68

music tracks to AutoMovie, 80

narration to videos, 122-124

normalized audio to video, 144-145

slideshows to DVD projects, 170-173

submenus to DVD projects, 169

titles, 96-97

titles between clips, 98-99

titles to clips, 100-101

video clips to Storyboard, 70-71

adjusting

contrast, 118

slideshow image display times, 155

Timeline view, 75

albums, creating, 152

analog camcorders, capturing video from, 51

analog connectors, 4

animated buttons, 164

applying

effects to still images, 156

tint, 119

archiving movies, 58-59

aspect ratios, 26, 41

switching between, 27

audio, 120

adding to AutoMovie, 80

audio effects, 127

clip-on microphones, 32

clips, dividing, 128

clips, muting, 128

clips, trimming, 133

customizing for DVD projects, 165

editing in Timeline, 74

eliminating silence, 133

exporting, 139

fading audio, 127

files, editing, 140

gain control, 32

J-cuts, 120, 134-135

L-cuts, 120, 136-137

layering, 136

levels, setting, 126

menu loop time, 165

microphones, 31

monitoring with headphones, 33

monitoring volume, 33

muting, 125

narration, 120-124

normalization, 120

normalized audio, adding to video, 144-145

normalized audio, editing, 145

normalizing, 142-143

sound tracks, creating, 129

volume, adjusting, 125

audio files, importing into Movie Maker, 130-131

audio levels, 126

AutoMovie, 78-81

customizing, 80-81

music tracks, adding, 80

muting video tracks, 81

previewing movies, 83

saving movies, 82-83

sharing movies via email, 82

time limits, 81

AutoMovie feature, 152

B

background music. *See audio; music*

batteries (camcorder), 12

black-and-white movies, 116

Brightness effects, 117

browsing folders, 42

burning

DVDs, 174-175

VCDs, 176-177

button frames (Sonic MyDVD), 164

buttons (Sonic MyDVD), 164

animated buttons, 164

C

camcorders

batteries, 12

connecting to PCs with FireWire, 38

connecting to PCs with S-Video, 39

connecting TV monitors to, 11

Digital8, connecting to PCs, 34

features of, 4-5

FireWire, 4

hoods to prevent glare, 10

one-CCD camcorders, 13

positioning, 17

remotes, 5

stabilizing, 17

still images, capturing, 5

three-CCD camcorders, 13

tripods, 6-7

zoom features, 8-9

capturing. *See also* **recording**

live video, 54-55

movie segments, 44-45

still images with camcorders, 5

video, 42-43.

video from analog camcorders, 51

video, reducing processor/memory usage, 43

video using zoom feature, 8-9

card readers, 149

CCDs (charged-coupled devices), 13

CD players, HighMAT format, 64

CDs, saving movies to, 64-65

chapter markers, 166

chapter titles, editing, 168

chapters

adding, 167

creating, 166-167

editing, 166-167

chapters menu, editing, 168

charged-coupled devices (CCDs), 13

clip-on microphones, 32

clips, 68. *See* **video clips**

audio, trimming, 133

organizing, 46

close-up shots, shooting, 22

Collections, removing, 72

color

correction, 119

enhancing, 117

combining movie clips, 85

compressing movies to share via email, 180-181

configuring Movie Maker, 40-41

connecting

camcorders to PCs using FireWire, 38

camcorders to PCs using S-Video, 39

Digital8 camcorders to PCs, 34

DV cameras to PCs, 148

TV monitors to camcorders, 11

contrast, adjusting, 118

copying video clips, 73

copyright issues, 129-130, 185

credit overlays, 103

credits, adding, 102-103

cross fades, 95

crowd shots, 25

custom titles, adding to movies, 114

customizing

AutoMovie, 80-81

DVD menus, 163

menu buttons, 164

cutaway shots, shooting, 25

deleting

clips from Timeline, 77

transitions, 91

video clips, 69

diffusing light, 30

digital artifacts, 28

digital movies, shooting, 14

digital zoom, 9

Digital8 camcorders, connecting to PCs, 34

directional dissolves, 92

dissolves, adding, 92-93

dividing movie clips, 84

DV camcorder LCD, 10

DV cameras

connecting to PCs, 148

connecting to VCRs, 62

saving movies, 58-59

saving movies to, 60-61

DV tapes, transferring movies from, 63

DVD menus

custom menu styles, creating, 163

customizing, 163

customizing audio, 165

menu text, modifying, 162

submenus, adding, 169

DVD players, HighMAT format, 64

DVD projects

chapters, adding, 167

chapters, creating, 166-167

custom menu soundtracks, adding, 165

DVD projects

inserting movies into projects, 161

menu text, modifying, 162

opening, 162

previewing, 174

saving, 162

slideshows, 170-173

submenus, adding, 169

transitions, turning on/off, 172

DVDs

burning, 174-175

creating, 161

Sonic MyDVD, 158

E

Easy Media Creator, 142-143

echo, eliminating, 123

editing

audio files, 140

chapter titles, 168

chapters, 166-167

chapters menu, 168

normalized audio, 145

soundtrack files, 142-143

video, 66

effects, 88

black-and-white, 116

Brightness effects, 117

Pixelan effects, 118

sepia tone, 116

SpiceFX packs, 88

Tone Cooler effect, 119

Tone Warmer effect, 119

Electronic Image Stabilizing (Steadyshot), 4

email

sending movies via, 82

sharing movies via, 180-181

establishing shots, shooting, 24

exporting

audio, 139

video, 56

extracting

still images from memory cards, 149

still images from video, 151

F

Fade In feature, 74

fade transitions, 94-95

fades

adding, 94-95

combining with J-cuts, 135

cross fades, 95

fading audio, 127

fading in/out, 75

files, organizing, 46

finding

    folders, 42

    photos for importing, 47

FireWire, 4, 38

    connecting camcorders to PCs, 38

    connecting Digital8 camcorders to PCs with, 34

    for notebook computers, 59

flash card readers, 149

folders, finding, 42

frames (hidden), 86

framing, 16

    headroom, 18

    nose room, 19

    shots, 4

full screen movies, aspect ratios, 41

Fun Packs, 88

G-H

gain control (audio), 32

HDTV playback, 26

headphones, monitoring audio using, 33

headroom, framing, 18

headset microphones, 123

Hi8 video, transferring, 34

hidden frames, 86

HighMAT format, 64

hot shoe, 5

I

I-link. *See* **FireWire**

IEEE 1394. *See* **FireWire**

image types supported by Movie Maker, 47

images, 148. *See also* **still images**

    organizing in slideshows, 171

importing

    custom titles into movies, 114

    music into Movie Maker, 130-131

    still images, 150

    still photos into movies, 47

    VHS movies with a USB device, 50-53

    video, 36-39

    video clips into movies, 68

increasing Timeline size, 75

inserting

    movies into DVD projects, 161

    transitions, 90-91

J-K-L

J-cuts, 120, 134-135
combining with fades, 135

L-cuts, 120, 136-137
launching Video Capture Wizard, 41
layering audio, 136
LCD viewfinders, 4, 10
lighting
natural lighting, 30
shadows, 30
live video
capturing, 54-55
testing audio, 54

M

medium close-up shots, shooting, 21
memory usage, reducing during video capture, 43
menu buttons, customizing, 164
menus (DVD), modifying menu text, 162

microphones, 31
clip-on microphones, 32
headset microphones, 123
Microsoft Paint
creating custom title slides, 105-109
creating custom titles, 104
Text Toolbar, displaying, 109
Microsoft PowerPoint
creating custom title slides, 110-113
Getting Started Task Pane, displaying, 110
slide layouts/designs library, 111
text boxes, moving, 112
monitoring
audio volume, 33
narration, 123
video recording, 10
Movie button, restoring, 167
movie clips
combining, 85
effects, adding to, 115
fades, adding, 94-95
organizing, 46
splitting, 84
transitions, inserting, 90-91
trimming, 86-87

Movie Maker

AutoMovie, customizing, 80-81

AutoMovie feature, 152

Collections, 46

configuring, 40-41

file format support, 146

Fun Packs, 88

image types (supported), 47

importing music into, 130-131

importing video clips, 68

live video, capturing, 54-55

projects, creating, 40

Save for the Web option, 182-183

saving movies, 60-61

special effects, 146

Storyboard, 66

Timeline, 66

Video Effect collection, 115

video, editing, 66

Movie Maker files

formats, 141

saving, 139

Movie Maker Storyboard, creating slideshows, 152

movies. *See also* video

adding custom title to, 114

black-and-white, 116

movie segments, capturing, 44-45

organizing files, 46

previewing in AutoMovie, 83

removing Collections from, 72

removing video clips from, 69

saving, 58-59, 63

saving in AutoMovie, 82-83

saving to CDs, 64-65

saving for Pocket PC playback, 188-189

scenes, dividing into, 43

sepia tone, 116

still photos, importing, 47

storing on the Web, 182-183

Timeline, 74

transferring to Pocket PCs, 190-191

transferring to VHS, 62

VHS, importing with a DV camera, 48-49

VHS, importing with a USB device, 50-53

video clips, adding, 68

widescreen, creating, 41

music

adding to AutoMovie, 80

adding to Timeline, 132

adding to video, 129

copyright issues, 129

importing into video, 130-131

muting

audio clips, 125, 128

video tracks, 81

MyDVD. *See* Sonic MyDVD

N

narrating slideshows, 154

narration, 120-124

echo, eliminating, 123

headset microphones, 123

monitoring, 123

slideshows, 154

Neptune Mediashare hosting service, 182

normalization, 120, 138-141

normalized audio, editing, 145

normalizing

audio, 142-143

soundtracks, 138-141

nose room, framing, 19

O

opening

DVD projects, 162

Sonic MyDVD, 160

optical zoom, 5

organizing

images in slideshows, 171

video clips, 70-71

video files, 46

O T S

OTS (over-the-shoulder) shots, shooting, 23

overlay titles, 101

P

Paint. *See* Microsoft Paint

Pan effects, 156-157

photo slideshows, creating, 152-155

photographs, archiving in Sonic MyDVD, 173

photos, 148. *See also* images

finding, 47

importing into movies, 47

pictures, 155. *See also* images

rotating in slideshows, 170

Pixelan effects, 118

color correction effects, 119

Pixelan Web site, 146

planning shots, 16

Pocket PCs

saving movies for playback, 188-189

transferring movies to, 190-191

portable devices, transferring movies to, 190-191

positioning camcorders, 17

PowerPoint. *See* Microsoft PowerPoint

previewing

DVD projects, 174

movies in AutoMovie, 83

processor usage, reducing during video capture, 43

R

recording

8mm projection movies with DV cameras, 35

movies, 60. *See also* saving, movies

movies to CDs, 64

movies from DV camera to VHS, 63

movies to VCR, 62

VHS to MiniDV, 48-49

removing. *See also* **trimming**

clips from Timeline, 77

Collections, 72

images from slideshows, 171

video clips, 69

video clips from Storyboard, 70-71

rendering process, 91

repeating video clips, 71

restoring Movie button, 167

rotating pictures in slideshows, 170

Roxio Easy Media Creator, 142-143

S

S-Video, connecting camcorders to PCs, 39

saving

DVD projects, 162

Movie Maker files, 139

movies, 58-59

movies in AutoMovie, 82-83

movies to CDs, 64-65

movies to DV cameras, 60-61

movies from DV tapes to VHS, 63

movies for email sharing, 180-181

movies for Pocket PC playback, 188-189

movies for the Web, 182-183

movies to the Web using SmartFTP, 184-187

sepia tone movies, 116

setting audio levels, 126

shadows (lighting), 30

sharing movies via email, 82, 180-181

shooting

close-up shots, 22

crowd shots, 25

cutaway shots, 25

digital movies, 14

establishing shots, 24

framing, 4

How can we make this index more useful? Email us at indexes@quepublishing.com

shooting

medium close-up shots, 21

OTS (over-the-shoulder) shots, 23

planning shots, 16

wide shots, 20, 24

slideshows

adding to DVD projects, 170-173

audio tracks, adding, 171

creating, 152-155

display time, adjusting, 155

images, organizing, 171

images, removing, 171

Movie Maker's AutoMovie feature, 152

narrating, 154

pictures, rotating, 170

SmartFTP, uploading movies to the Web, 184-187

songs. *See* **audio**

Sonic MyDVD, 158

archiving photos, 173

buttons, 164

menus, 163

opening, 160

slideshows, generating, 170

soundtracks, 120. *See also* **audio**

adding to DVD projects, 165

creating, 129

editing, 142-143

normalized soundtracks, adding to video, 144-145

normalized soundtracks, editing, 145

normalizing, 138-141

SpiceFX packs, 88, 146

splitting

movie clips, 84

movie clips on the Timeline, 84

stabilizing camcorders, 17

Steadyshot, 4

Still Camera Mode, 5

still images (photos), 5, 146

creating from video, 151

effects, apply to, 156

extracting from memory cards, 148-149

importing, 150

motion, adding to, 156-157

Pan effects, 156-157

slideshows, creating, 152-155

Zoom effects, 156-157

stills. *See* **still images**

storing movies on the Web, 182-183

Storyboard, 66

adding clip collections to, 71

adding video clips, 70-71

copying clips, 73

removing video clips, 70-71

storyboards, 152

streaming video, 178

> saving movies to the Web, 182-183

submenus, adding to DVD projects, 169

subtitles, 98

Super8 film, 35

T

text box backgrounds, creating, 107

Timeline, 66, 74

> adding music to, 132
>
> adding video clips to, 76
>
> fading, 75
>
> increasing size of, 75
>
> overlay titles, adding, 101
>
> removing clips from, 77
>
> splitting movie clips, 84
>
> video clips, repeating, 76

tint, applying, 119

title slides, custom backgrounds, creating, 113

titles, 88

> adding, 96-97
>
> adding between clips, 98-99

adding to clips, 100-101

> custom titles, adding to movies, 114
>
> custom titles, creating in Microsoft Paint, 104-109
>
> custom titles, creating in PowerPoint, 110-113
>
> overlay titles, 101
>
> subtitles, 98

Tone Cooler effect, 119

Tone Warmer effect, 119

tracks (audio), muting, 128

transferring

> Hi8 video, 34
>
> movies to Pocket PCs, 190-191
>
> video, 4

transitions, 88

> deleting, 91
>
> dissolves, adding, 92-93
>
> duration (default), 95
>
> fades, 94-95
>
> inserting, 90-91
>
> SpiceFX packs, 88
>
> turning on/off, 172

trimming

> audio clips, 133
>
> movie clips, 86-87

tripods, 6-7

> leveling bubbles, 6
>
> pan handles, 6

tripods

panning, 6

quick release plates, 7

telescoping legs, 7

tilting, 6

TV tuner cards, 53

U-V

unhiding Movie button, 167

uploading movies to the Web, 184-187

VCDs, 65, 158

burning, 176-177

VCRs, connecting DV cameras to, 62

VHS

saving movies to, 63

transferring movies to, 62

VHS movies

importing with a DV camera, 48-49

importing with a USB device, 50-51, 53

video. *See also* movies

capturing, 42-43

creating still images from, 151

editing, 66

exporting, 56

importing, 36-39

live video, capturing, 54-55

music, adding, 129

narration, adding, 122-124

organizing files, 46

shooting in 16:9, 26

shooting in 4:3, 27

streaming, 178

transferring, 4

zooming in/out, 8-9

Video Capture Wizard, launching, 41

video clips

adding to movies, 68

adding to Timeline, 76

collections, adding to Storyboard, 71

copying, 73

importing, 68

organizing, 70-71

preparing for AutoMovie, 78-79

recovering deleted clips, 69

removing, 69

repeating, 71

Video Effect collection (Windows Movie Maker), 115

video framing, 16

video recording

lighting, 30

monitoring, 10-11

video tracks, muting, 81

volume, adjusting, 125

W

Web

saving movie for, 182-183

uploading movies to using SmartFTP, 184-187

Webcams

capturing live video, 54-55

facial recognition, turning off, 55

wide shots, 24

shooting, 20

widescreen movies, aspect ratios, 41

Windows Media Player, extracting music from CDs, 129

Windows Movie Maker, 120

AutoMovie, customizing, 80-81

AutoMovie feature, 152

Collections, 46

configuring, 40-41

file format support, 146

Fun Packs, 88

image types (supported), 47

importing music into, 130-131

importing video clips, 68

live video, capturing, 54-55

projects, creating, 40

Save for the Web option, 182-183

saving movies, 60-61

special effects, 146

Storyboard, 66

Timeline, 66

Video Effect collection, 115

video, editing, 66

wizards, Video Capture Wizard, 41

wma file format, 141

write speeds, 175

X-Y-Z

Zoom effects, 156-157

zoom feature, 8-9

Rather than having you read through a lot of text, Easy lets you learn visually. Users are introduced to topics of technology, hardware, software, and computers in a friendly, yet motivating, manner.

Easy Digital Cameras

Mark Edward Soper
ISBN: 0-7897-3077-4
$19.99 USA/$28.99 CAN

Easy Creating CDs & DVDs

Tom Bunzel
ISBN: 0-7897-2972-5
$19.99 USA/$30.99 CAN

Easy Windows® XP, Home Edition, Second Edition

Shelley O'Hara
Kate Shoup Welsh
ISBN: 0-7897-3036-7
$19.99 USA/$30.99 CAN

Easy Microsoft® Office 2003

Nancy Warner
ISBN: 0-7897-2962-8
$14.99 USA/$22.99 CAN

Special offer!

Save 25% on Easy Digital Cameras

Easy Digital Cameras is the perfect book to help you learn to take pristine pictures using all the features of your digital camera. Then it shows you how to edit them for perfection and share them with your friends and family (whether you print them, burn them to a CD, or share them online via email or the Web).

Purchasers of *Easy Digital Home Movies* get three chapters from *Easy Digital Cameras* on this CD, and a special discount of 25% off the purchase of *Easy Digital Cameras*! To get your discount, go to www.quepublishing.com, look up *Easy Digital Cameras*, enter discount code ESYCAM when prompted at checkout, and you will get a 25% discount and free shipping! Take advantage of this special offer today.

Offer expires January 15, 2005.

License Agreement

Microsoft Software